THERAVADA BUDDHISM FOR BEGINNERS

UNDERSTANDING THE CORE TEACHINGS

LAUREN CHRISTENSEN

Copyright © 2024 by Lauren Christensen

All rights reserved.

No part of this book may be reproduced in any form or by any electronic or mechanical means, including information storage and retrieval systems, without written permission from the author, except for the use of brief quotations in a book review.

For my Family

Do not dwell in the past, do not dream of the future, concentrate the mind on the present moment.

— BUDDHA

CONTENTS

Introduction xi

1. HISTORICAL CONTEXT AND DEVELOPMENT 1
   Pre-Buddhist Indian Context 1
   Life of Siddhartha Gautama 3
   Early Buddhist Councils 4
   Spread to Sri Lanka 6
   Influence in Southeast Asia 7
   Modern Revival Movements 9
   Theravada in the Western World 11

2. CORE TEACHINGS AND DOCTRINES 13
   The Four Noble Truths 13
   The Noble Eightfold Path 15
   The Three Marks of Existence 16
   Dependent Origination 18
   Karma and Rebirth 19
   The Concept of Nibbana (Nirvana) 21
   The Five Aggregates (Skandhas) 22

3. THE PALI CANON 25
   Vinaya Pitaka 25
   Sutta Pitaka 27
   Abhidhamma Pitaka 28
   Compilation and Preservation 30
   Key Texts and Commentaries 31
   Language and Style 33
   Importance in Daily Practice 35

4. MONASTIC LIFE AND THE SANGHA 37
   Ordination Process 37
   Daily Routine of Monks and Nuns 39
   Monastic Rules and Discipline 40
   Role of the Sangha in the Community 42

Monastic Education and Training	43
Lay Support and Dana (Generosity)	45
Challenges and Adaptations	46

5. MEDITATION PRACTICES — 49
   - Importance of Meditation in Theravada — 49
   - Samatha (Calm) Meditation — 50
   - Vipassana (Insight) Meditation — 52
   - Common Meditation Techniques — 53
   - Role of Meditation Retreats — 55
   - Benefits and Challenges — 56
   - Integration with Daily Life — 58

6. RITUALS AND FESTIVALS — 61
   - Major Theravada Festivals — 61
   - Rituals for Birth, Marriage, and Death — 63
   - Daily and Weekly Devotional Practices — 64
   - Role of Temples and Stupas — 66
   - Pilgrimage Sites — 67
   - Cultural Variations in Rituals — 69
   - Contemporary Adaptations — 70

7. ETHICAL CONDUCT AND PRECEPTS — 73
   - The Five Precepts for Lay Buddhists — 73
   - The Eight Precepts — 75
   - The Ten Precepts for Novices — 76
   - The Role of Sila (Morality) in Practice — 78
   - Ethical Challenges in Modern Times — 80
   - The Impact of Ethical Conduct on Society — 81

8. THERAVADA IN DIFFERENT CULTURES — 84
   - Theravada in Sri Lanka — 84
   - Theravada in Thailand — 86
   - Theravada in Myanmar (Burma) — 87
   - Theravada in Cambodia and Laos — 88
   - Theravada in Other Parts of the World — 90
   - Cultural Influences and Adaptations — 91
   - Comparative Study with Other Buddhist Traditions — 93

9. WOMEN IN THERAVADA BUDDHISM — 95
   Historical Role of Women — 95
   Ordination of Women — 96
   Notable Female Practitioners and Teachers — 98
   Challenges Faced by Women in the Sangha — 100
   Modern Movements for Gender Equality — 101
   Contributions of Women to Theravada — 103
   Future Prospects — 104

10. CONTEMPORARY ISSUES AND FUTURE DIRECTIONS — 107
   Theravada and Modern Science — 107
   Socially Engaged Buddhism — 109
   Environmental Ethics in Theravada — 110
   Interfaith Dialogue and Cooperation — 112
   Theravada and Globalization — 114
   Preserving Tradition in the Modern World — 116
   Vision for the Future — 117

Conclusion — 121
Glossary — 133
Suggested Readings — 139

INTRODUCTION

ORIGINS OF THERAVADA BUDDHISM

Theravada Buddhism traces its roots to the teachings of Siddhartha Gautama, who lived and taught in the 5th century BCE. Born a prince in what is now Nepal, Gautama renounced his royal life to seek enlightenment. After years of ascetic practices and meditation, he attained enlightenment under the Bodhi tree in Bodh Gaya, India. His insights into the nature of suffering and the path to its cessation became the foundation of Theravada Buddhism.

The term "Theravada" means "Teaching of the Elders," reflecting its adherence to the earliest teachings of the Buddha. These teachings were preserved by his closest disciples and passed down through generations. Theravada is considered the oldest form of Buddhism, maintaining a direct lineage to the original teachings of the Buddha. This historical continuity is a hallmark of Theravada and distinguishes it from other Buddhist traditions.

INTRODUCTION

Initially, the teachings of the Buddha were transmitted orally. Monks and nuns memorized his discourses and recited them in communal gatherings. This oral tradition ensured the preservation of the teachings until they were eventually written down. The written records, known as the Pali Canon, became the cornerstone of Theravada practice and study. The meticulous preservation of these texts underscores the importance of accuracy and fidelity to the original teachings in Theravada Buddhism.

The spread of Theravada Buddhism began shortly after the Buddha's death. Missionaries were sent to various regions, including Sri Lanka, where Theravada established a stronghold. The teachings adapted to different cultures while maintaining their core principles. This ability to remain true to the original teachings while adapting to new contexts contributed to the resilience and longevity of Theravada Buddhism.

Throughout its history, Theravada has faced challenges and undergone transformations. Political upheavals, cultural shifts, and internal reforms have all shaped its development. Despite these changes, the core principles of Theravada have remained intact, providing a stable foundation for its followers. This stability has allowed Theravada Buddhism to thrive and continue its mission of guiding individuals toward enlightenment.

KEY FIGURES IN EARLY THERAVADA HISTORY

The early history of Theravada Buddhism is marked by the contributions of several key figures who played pivotal roles in its development and dissemination. One of the most

INTRODUCTION

significant figures is Ananda, the Buddha's cousin and personal attendant. Ananda's exceptional memory and dedication to preserving the Buddha's teachings were instrumental in the formation of the Pali Canon. His efforts ensured that the Buddha's discourses were accurately recorded and transmitted to future generations.

Another important figure is Mahinda, the son of Emperor Ashoka, who was a devoted follower of the Buddha. Mahinda is credited with introducing Theravada Buddhism to Sri Lanka in the 3rd century BCE. His mission to Sri Lanka laid the foundation for the establishment of Theravada as the dominant form of Buddhism on the island. Mahinda's efforts were complemented by those of his sister, Sanghamitta, who brought the first branch of the sacred Bodhi tree to Sri Lanka, further solidifying the presence of Theravada Buddhism.

Emperor Ashoka himself is a key figure in the history of Theravada Buddhism. After converting to Buddhism, Ashoka became a fervent supporter of the religion, promoting its teachings throughout his empire and beyond. His patronage and support helped to spread Theravada Buddhism to various regions, including Sri Lanka and Southeast Asia. Ashoka's commitment to non-violence and moral governance also influenced the development of Buddhist ethics and social values.

The first Buddhist council, held shortly after the Buddha's death, was another crucial event in the early history of Theravada. Convened by Mahakasyapa, one of the Buddha's foremost disciples, the council aimed to compile and preserve the Buddha's teachings. The recitations and discussions that

INTRODUCTION

took place during the council formed the basis of the Pali Canon. The success of this council ensured the continuity and integrity of the teachings for future generations.

Subsequent Buddhist councils played significant roles in the preservation and clarification of the teachings. The second council, held approximately a century after the first, addressed issues of monastic discipline and doctrinal disputes. These early councils were critical in establishing the foundations of Theravada Buddhism and ensuring the purity and consistency of its teachings.

BASIC BELIEFS AND PRACTICES

Theravada Buddhism is grounded in a set of core beliefs and practices that guide the spiritual journey of its followers. Central to these beliefs is the understanding of the Four Noble Truths, which form the foundation of the Buddha's teachings. The first truth acknowledges the existence of suffering in life; the second identifies desire and attachment as the causes of suffering; the third asserts that the cessation of suffering is possible, and the fourth outlines the path to the cessation of suffering, known as the Noble Eightfold Path.

The Noble Eightfold Path is a comprehensive guide to ethical conduct, mental discipline, and wisdom. It encompasses right understanding, right intention, right speech, right action, right livelihood, right effort, right mindfulness, and right concentration. Each aspect of the path contributes to the development of moral character, mental clarity, and insight, ultimately leading to the attainment of enlightenment, or nibbana.

INTRODUCTION

Meditation is a key practice in Theravada Buddhism, serving as a tool for developing mindfulness and insight. There are two primary types of meditation: samatha, or calm abiding, and vipassana, or insight meditation. Samatha meditation focuses on developing concentration and tranquility, often through the practice of focusing on a single object, such as the breath. Vipassana meditation, on the other hand, aims to cultivate insight into the true nature of reality by observing the impermanent and interconnected nature of all phenomena.

Ethical conduct, or sila, is another fundamental aspect of Theravada practice. Followers are encouraged to adhere to a set of precepts that promote non-harming, honesty, and self-restraint. For lay Buddhists, these precepts typically include refraining from killing, stealing, sexual misconduct, lying, and intoxication. Monastics observe additional precepts that govern their conduct and interactions with the lay community, ensuring a life of simplicity and discipline.

The practice of dana, or generosity, is also highly valued in Theravada Buddhism. Dana involves giving and sharing with others, particularly the monastic community, as an expression of selflessness and compassion. This practice not only supports the livelihood of monks and nuns but also cultivates a sense of interconnectedness and mutual support within the community. Through these beliefs and practices, Theravada Buddhists strive to lead lives of moral integrity, mental clarity, and spiritual insight.

THE PALI CANON

The Pali Canon, also known as the Tipitaka, is the authoritative scripture of Theravada Buddhism. It is divided into

INTRODUCTION

three main sections: the Vinaya Pitaka, the Sutta Pitaka, and the Abhidhamma Pitaka. The Vinaya Pitaka contains the rules and regulations governing monastic conduct, ensuring the proper discipline and ethical behavior of monks and nuns. It provides detailed guidelines on various aspects of monastic life, including ordination procedures, daily routines, and interactions with the lay community.

The Sutta Pitaka is a collection of discourses attributed to the Buddha and his close disciples. It encompasses a wide range of teachings, from practical advice on ethical living to profound philosophical discussions. The suttas are organized into several sub-collections, including the Digha Nikaya (Long Discourses), Majjhima Nikaya (Middle-Length Discourses), Samyutta Nikaya (Connected Discourses), Anguttara Nikaya (Numerical Discourses), and Khuddaka Nikaya (Minor Collection). Each sub-collection serves a unique purpose, addressing different aspects of the Buddha's teachings.

The Abhidhamma Pitaka is a systematic analysis of the Buddha's teachings, presenting them in a highly detailed and technical manner. It explores the nature of mind and matter, the process of cognition, and the classification of mental and physical phenomena. The Abhidhamma provides a framework for understanding the intricate workings of the mind and the interdependent nature of reality, offering advanced practitioners a deeper level of insight into the teachings.

The Pali Canon was initially preserved through oral transmission, with monks and nuns memorizing and reciting the texts. This oral tradition ensured the accuracy and integrity of the teachings before they were eventually written down.

INTRODUCTION

The written compilation of the Pali Canon took place in Sri Lanka during the first century BCE, a monumental effort that involved the collaboration of numerous scholars and scribes. This written record has since become the foundation of Theravada study and practice.

The Pali language, in which the Canon is written, holds great significance in Theravada Buddhism. It is considered the language of the earliest Buddhist scriptures and is closely associated with the historical Buddha. The study of Pali enables practitioners to engage directly with the original texts, fostering a deeper understanding of the teachings. The preservation and study of the Pali Canon remain central to the Theravada tradition, providing a rich source of guidance and inspiration for followers.

DISTINCTIVE FEATURES OF THERAVADA

Theravada Buddhism is characterized by several distinctive features that set it apart from other Buddhist traditions. One of the most notable features is its emphasis on the original teachings of the Buddha, as preserved in the Pali Canon. This adherence to the earliest scriptures ensures a direct connection to the historical Buddha's teachings, maintaining their purity and authenticity. Theravada practitioners place great importance on studying and understanding these texts, viewing them as the authoritative source of guidance on the path to enlightenment.

Another distinctive feature of Theravada is its focus on the individual practitioner's journey toward enlightenment. While community and monastic life are highly valued, the ultimate goal is personal liberation from the cycle of birth and death (samsara). This emphasis on individual effort is reflected in the practice of meditation, ethical conduct, and the cultivation of wisdom. Each practitioner is encouraged to take responsibility for their spiritual development, working diligently to overcome ignorance and achieve insight.

Theravada Buddhism places a strong emphasis on monastic life and the role of the Sangha (monastic community). Monks and nuns are seen as the living embodiments of the Buddha's teachings, serving as teachers, guides, and exemplars of the Buddhist path. The monastic community plays a vital role in preserving and transmitting the teachings, offering support and guidance to lay practitioners. The relationship between the monastic and lay communities is characterized by mutual respect and support, with laypeople providing material support and monastics offering spiritual guidance.

The concept of "arahant" is central to Theravada Buddhism, representing an individual who has attained enlightenment and achieved liberation from samsara. The arahant serves as a model for practitioners, demonstrating the potential for personal transformation and the attainment of nibbana. This focus on the arahant contrasts with other Buddhist traditions that emphasize the bodhisattva ideal, in which individuals postpone their own enlightenment to help others achieve liberation.

Theravada Buddhism is also distinguished by its strong emphasis on meditation and mindfulness practices. These practices are seen as essential tools for developing concentration, insight, and wisdom. Meditation retreats and centers

INTRODUCTION

are widespread in Theravada countries, providing opportunities for intensive practice and spiritual growth. The focus on meditation and mindfulness reflects Theravada's commitment to experiential understanding and direct realization of the Buddha's teachings.

GEOGRAPHICAL SPREAD OF THERAVADA BUDDHISM

Theravada Buddhism has a rich history of geographical spread, reaching various regions and cultures over the centuries. Its journey began in India, where the Buddha first taught his doctrines. From there, Theravada Buddhism spread to Sri Lanka in the 3rd century BCE, a significant milestone in its history. The island nation became a stronghold for Theravada, with its teachings deeply influencing the culture, politics, and social life of the region. Sri Lanka played a crucial role in preserving the Pali Canon and maintaining the Theravada tradition.

As Theravada Buddhism took root in Sri Lanka, it began to expand further into Southeast Asia. By the 11th century CE, it had reached Burma (Myanmar), where it was embraced as the state religion. The Burmese people incorporated Theravada teachings into their daily lives, and the monastic community flourished. The spread of Theravada continued into Thailand, Cambodia, and Laos, where it became the dominant form of Buddhism, shaping the cultural and religious landscape of these countries.

In each of these regions, Theravada Buddhism adapted to local customs and traditions while maintaining its core teachings. This adaptability allowed it to thrive in diverse cultural contexts, fostering a rich tapestry of practices and expressions. Local festivals, rituals, and artistic expressions of Theravada Buddhism reflect the unique cultural influences of each region, while the foundational teachings of the Buddha remain unchanged.

In more recent times, Theravada Buddhism has spread beyond Asia to other parts of the world, including Europe, North America, and Australia. This global expansion has been facilitated by increased travel, communication, and the efforts of dedicated teachers and practitioners. As Theravada Buddhism reaches new audiences, it continues to adapt to contemporary contexts, addressing the needs and concerns of modern practitioners.

The geographical spread of Theravada Buddhism has been marked by both challenges and opportunities. Political changes, economic pressures, and cultural shifts have all influenced its development and dissemination. Despite these challenges, Theravada Buddhism remains a vital and vibrant tradition, offering guidance and inspiration to millions of followers worldwide. Its enduring appeal lies in its ability to speak to the universal human experience, providing a path to peace, wisdom, and liberation.

CONTEMPORARY RELEVANCE AND PRACTICE

In today's fast-paced and interconnected world, Theravada Buddhism continues to offer valuable insights and practices that resonate with people seeking meaning and fulfillment. One of its key contributions is the emphasis on mindfulness and meditation, which have gained widespread popularity in recent years. Mindfulness practices, derived from Theravada

INTRODUCTION

traditions, are now used in various contexts, including healthcare, education, and business, to promote well-being, focus, and emotional resilience.

Theravada Buddhism also addresses contemporary ethical and social issues through its teachings on compassion, non-violence, and interdependence. These principles provide a framework for addressing challenges such as environmental degradation, social injustice, and conflict resolution. By encouraging individuals to act with kindness and integrity, Theravada Buddhism fosters a sense of responsibility and interconnectedness that extends beyond the individual to encompass the broader community and environment.

The practice of dana, or generosity, remains a vital aspect of contemporary Theravada practice, fostering a culture of giving and support within communities. Laypeople provide material support to the monastic community, while monks and nuns offer spiritual guidance and teachings. This reciprocal relationship strengthens the bonds between individuals and communities, promoting a sense of unity and shared purpose.

Theravada Buddhism continues to adapt to modern contexts, addressing the needs and concerns of contemporary practitioners. New meditation centers, online resources, and educational programs provide access to the teachings and practices of Theravada Buddhism, making them more accessible to people around the world. This adaptability ensures that Theravada remains relevant and meaningful in today's rapidly changing world.

The enduring appeal of Theravada Buddhism lies in its ability to provide practical guidance for navigating the chal-

INTRODUCTION

lenges of modern life. Its teachings offer a path to personal transformation, encouraging individuals to cultivate mindfulness, compassion, and wisdom. As more people seek to integrate these values into their lives, Theravada Buddhism continues to inspire and support individuals on their spiritual journey toward peace and enlightenment.

HISTORICAL CONTEXT AND DEVELOPMENT

PRE-BUDDHIST INDIAN CONTEXT

Long before Buddhism emerged, ancient India was a land of diverse spiritual practices and philosophical inquiry. The Vedic tradition, which later evolved into Hinduism, dominated the religious landscape. It centered around rituals, sacrifices, and hymns dedicated to various deities, reflecting a belief system that placed great emphasis on the cosmic order and societal hierarchy. The Brahmins, as priests, were the keepers of sacred knowledge, performing complex ceremonies that maintained the balance between humans and the divine.

Amidst this religious framework, a new wave of thinkers began to question the established order. These were the sramanas, or seekers, who rejected the authority of the Vedas and the rigid social structure. They sought enlightenment through meditation, ascetic practices, and philosophical inquiry, exploring ideas about the nature of reality and the self. The sramanas' search for truth paved the way for new spiritual movements, including Buddhism and Jainism, which offered alternative paths to spiritual liberation.

The sramana tradition emerged in response to the limitations of the Vedic system. Unlike the Brahmins, who focused on external rituals, the sramanas emphasized personal experience and insight. They advocated for an inward journey, encouraging individuals to look beyond the material world and seek understanding through meditation and self-discipline. This shift from ritualistic practices to introspection marked a significant turning point in Indian spirituality.

The social and political climate of ancient India also influenced the development of new religious ideas. The rise of cities and trade brought people from different cultures and backgrounds together, creating a melting pot of ideas. This dynamic environment fostered intellectual exchange and debate as people sought new ways to understand the complexities of life. The teachings of the Buddha, with their emphasis on personal experience and ethical living, resonated with those seeking a deeper understanding of existence.

As these spiritual movements gained momentum, they challenged the traditional authority of the Vedic priests and the caste system. The sramanas, with their focus on individual liberation, offered a new vision of spiritual equality and personal responsibility. This radical departure from the established order laid the groundwork for the emergence of Buddhism, which would transform the religious landscape of India and beyond.

LIFE OF SIDDHARTHA GAUTAMA

Siddhartha Gautama, who would later become known as the Buddha, was born into a royal family in the Shakya clan in what is now Nepal. His early life was one of privilege and luxury, shielded from the hardships of the world outside the palace walls. His father, King Suddhodana, sought to protect him from the harsh realities of life, hoping to groom him to become a great ruler. However, Siddhartha's curiosity and desire to understand the world would lead him on a different path.

As Siddhartha grew older, he became increasingly aware of the suffering and impermanence that permeated existence. On a series of outings from the palace, he encountered the stark realities of old age, sickness, and death. These experiences profoundly affected him, igniting a deep yearning to find a way to overcome the suffering that seemed inherent to life. Siddhartha's encounters with these realities marked the beginning of his spiritual journey.

Driven by his quest for understanding, Siddhartha renounced his royal life at the age of 29. Leaving behind his family and the comforts of the palace, he embarked on a journey to seek enlightenment. He studied with various spiritual teachers, mastering their teachings and practices. However, despite his dedication, Siddhartha realized that these paths did not lead to the answers he sought. His dissatisfaction with traditional practices led him to explore new approaches to spiritual development.

Siddhartha's journey eventually led him to the practice of extreme asceticism, believing that self-denial could lead to enlightenment. He subjected himself to severe physical hardships, enduring long periods of fasting and meditation. Yet, even in the depths of ascetic practice, Siddhartha found no relief from suffering. This realization prompted him to abandon asceticism and seek a more balanced approach to spiritual practice, one that embraced moderation and inner reflection.

Under the Bodhi tree in Bodh Gaya, Siddhartha finally achieved enlightenment after a night of deep meditation. He realized the profound truths about the nature of suffering and the path to liberation, insights that would form the foundation of his teachings. Emerging as the Buddha, or "The Awakened One," he spent the remainder of his life sharing his insights with others, guiding them on the path to enlightenment. His teachings, known as the Dharma, would lay the groundwork for the spread of Buddhism across Asia and beyond.

EARLY BUDDHIST COUNCILS

Following the Buddha's death, his disciples faced the daunting task of preserving and transmitting his teachings. The first Buddhist council was convened shortly after his death to compile and organize his teachings, ensuring their authenticity and accuracy. This council was held in Rajagaha (modern-day Rajgir, India) under the leadership of Mahakasyapa, one of the Buddha's closest disciples. The recitations and discussions that took place during the council laid the foundation for the Pali Canon.

At the first council, the teachings were divided into three categories: the Vinaya (monastic rules), the Sutta (discourses), and the Abhidhamma (philosophical analyses). Ananda, the Buddha's cousin and personal attendant, played a crucial role in this process, relying on his exceptional memory to recite the Buddha's discourses. Upali, another key disciple, recited the Vinaya, ensuring that the monastic rules were preserved in their original form. The efforts of these disciples ensured the continuity of the Buddha's teachings for future generations.

A century later, the second Buddhist council was held in Vaisali (modern-day Vaishali, India) to address issues of monastic discipline and doctrinal disputes. The council was convened in response to disagreements regarding the interpretation and practice of monastic rules. Some monks sought to relax certain rules, leading to tensions within the monastic community. The council reaffirmed the original Vinaya and addressed the disputes, ensuring the unity and integrity of the Sangha (monastic community).

The third Buddhist council, convened under the patronage of Emperor Ashoka in the 3rd century BCE, played a significant role in the spread of Buddhism beyond India. This council aimed to purify the Sangha by expelling corrupt and heretical monks, as well as to compile a definitive version of the teachings. The council's efforts contributed to the dissemination of Buddhism throughout Ashoka's vast empire, as missionaries were sent to various regions to share the teachings.

These early councils were instrumental in establishing the foundations of Theravada Buddhism. They ensured the preservation and transmission of the Buddha's teachings, maintaining their authenticity and consistency. The councils also fostered a sense of unity and continuity within the monastic community, enabling Buddhism to thrive and adapt to changing times and contexts. Through their efforts, the early disciples laid the groundwork for the enduring legacy of Theravada Buddhism.

SPREAD TO SRI LANKA

The spread of Theravada Buddhism to Sri Lanka is a significant chapter in its history, marked by the efforts of Emperor Ashoka and his son Mahinda. In the 3rd century BCE, Ashoka, a devout supporter of Buddhism, dispatched missionaries to various regions to share the teachings of the Buddha. Mahinda, accompanied by a group of monks, arrived in Sri Lanka, where he was warmly received by King Devanampiya Tissa. This encounter marked the beginning of Theravada Buddhism's establishment on the island.

Mahinda's mission to Sri Lanka was a resounding success, as the king and many of his subjects embraced the teachings of the Buddha. The conversion of the royal family paved the way for the widespread acceptance of Buddhism, which quickly became the dominant religion on the island. Mahinda's teachings emphasized the importance of the Pali Canon, monastic discipline, and meditation practices, laying the foundation for a thriving Buddhist community.

The arrival of Sanghamitta, Mahinda's sister, further solidified the presence of Theravada Buddhism in Sri Lanka. She brought with her a sapling of the sacred Bodhi tree under which the Buddha had attained enlightenment. The planting of the Bodhi tree in Anuradhapura, the capital of Sri Lanka, became a symbol of the island's deep connection to the Buddha's teachings. The tree, known as the Sri Maha Bodhi, continues to be a revered site for Buddhists worldwide.

The establishment of monasteries and the construction of stupas played a crucial role in the spread of Buddhism throughout Sri Lanka. Monastic centers such as Mahavihara in Anuradhapura became hubs of learning and spiritual practice, attracting scholars and practitioners from across the region. These institutions served as repositories of Buddhist knowledge and played a vital role in preserving the Pali Canon and developing commentaries and interpretations of the teachings.

Theravada Buddhism's influence on Sri Lankan culture, politics, and society has been profound and enduring. It shaped the island's art, architecture, literature, and social values, fostering a rich cultural heritage that continues to thrive today. The spread of Theravada Buddhism to Sri Lanka laid the groundwork for its expansion to other parts of Southeast Asia, where it would continue to flourish and adapt to new contexts.

INFLUENCE IN SOUTHEAST ASIA

The influence of Theravada Buddhism in Southeast Asia is a testament to its adaptability and enduring appeal. As the teachings spread from Sri Lanka to regions such as Myanmar (Burma), Thailand, Cambodia, and Laos, they were embraced by diverse cultures and integrated into local traditions. The establishment of Theravada as the dominant form of Buddhism in these countries has had a profound impact on their cultural, social, and religious landscapes.

In Myanmar, Theravada Buddhism became the state religion during the reign of King Anawrahta in the 11th century CE. Anawrahta's conversion to Buddhism marked a turning point in the country's history as he sought to unify his kingdom under the teachings of the Buddha. The construction of pagodas and monasteries flourished, and the Pali Canon was studied and revered. The Burmese people integrated Theravada teachings into their daily lives, shaping their values and social structures.

Thailand's adoption of Theravada Buddhism followed a similar trajectory, with the religion becoming the cornerstone of Thai identity and culture. The kings of the Sukhothai and Ayutthaya kingdoms played pivotal roles in promoting Buddhism, supporting the construction of temples, and the establishment of monastic communities. Thai society embraced the principles of dana (generosity), sila (ethical conduct), and bhavana (meditation), integrating them into the fabric of daily life.

In Cambodia and Laos, Theravada Buddhism became deeply intertwined with the cultural and political spheres. The influence of Theravada teachings can be seen in the intricate carvings of Angkor Wat and the daily rituals of Lao monks. The monastic community played a central role in education and social welfare, serving as both spiritual guides and community leaders. The values of compassion, mindfulness, and ethical living continue to shape the cultural identity of these nations.

Throughout Southeast Asia, Theravada Buddhism has demonstrated a remarkable ability to adapt to local customs while maintaining its core teachings. This adaptability has allowed it to thrive in diverse cultural contexts, fostering a rich tapestry of practices and expressions. The influence of Theravada Buddhism in Southeast Asia extends beyond religious life, shaping art, architecture, music, and literature, and contributing to the region's unique cultural heritage.

Today, Theravada Buddhism continues to be a vital and vibrant tradition in Southeast Asia. Its teachings offer a path to spiritual fulfillment and ethical living, resonating with people seeking meaning and purpose in an ever-changing world. The enduring influence of Theravada Buddhism in Southeast Asia is a testament to its ability to address the universal human experience and provide a timeless guide to peace and wisdom.

MODERN REVIVAL MOVEMENTS

The modern revival of Theravada Buddhism has been shaped by a series of dynamic movements that seek to revitalize the tradition and address contemporary challenges. In the late 19th and early 20th centuries, reform movements emerged in response to colonial influences and the need to adapt to a rapidly changing world. These movements aimed to purify the monastic community, promote education, and engage with modern scientific and philosophical ideas.

One of the most influential figures in the revival of Theravada Buddhism was King Mongkut of Thailand, who reigned from 1851 to 1868. Before becoming king, Mongkut spent 27 years as a monk, during which he observed the need for reform within the Sangha. As king, he initiated a series of reforms that emphasized the study of the Pali Canon, the practice of meditation, and the adherence to monastic discipline. His efforts laid the foundation for a more rigorous and scholarly approach to Theravada practice.

In Sri Lanka, the revival of Theravada Buddhism was driven by figures such as Anagarika Dharmapala, who sought to restore the island's Buddhist heritage and counter the influence of Western colonial powers. Dharmapala emphasized the importance of education, social reform, and the global dissemination of Buddhist teachings. His efforts contributed to the establishment of Buddhist schools, the revival of ancient pilgrimage sites, and the promotion of interfaith dialogue.

The Vipassana movement, which gained momentum in the mid-20th century, has played a significant role in the modern revival of Theravada Buddhism. Vipassana, or insight meditation, emphasizes the development of mindfulness and awareness of the present moment. Teachers such as S.N. Goenka and Mahasi Sayadaw have popularized Vipassana meditation through courses and retreats, attracting practitioners from around the world. The movement's emphasis on experiential understanding and personal insight resonates with modern seekers.

Contemporary revival movements continue to address the challenges facing Theravada Buddhism in the modern world. Issues such as gender equality, environmental sustainability, and social justice are being explored within the framework of Buddhist teachings. Monastic and lay communities are engaging with these issues, seeking to integrate the principles of compassion, wisdom, and ethical conduct into responses to global challenges.

The modern revival of Theravada Buddhism reflects the tradition's resilience and adaptability. By engaging with contemporary issues and embracing new perspectives, Theravada Buddhism remains a relevant and dynamic force in the modern world. The efforts of revival movements ensure that the teachings of the Buddha continue to inspire and guide individuals on their spiritual journey, offering a path to peace, understanding, and transformation.

THERAVADA IN THE WESTERN WORLD

The introduction of Theravada Buddhism to the Western world is a relatively recent development, marked by a growing interest in meditation, mindfulness, and Eastern philosophy. The 20th century saw an increase in cross-cultural exchange as Western travelers, scholars, and spiritual seekers encountered Theravada teachings in Southeast Asia. This exchange laid the groundwork for the establishment of Theravada centers and communities in Europe, North America, and beyond.

The spread of Theravada Buddhism in the West has been facilitated by a diverse group of teachers and practitioners. Monks and nuns from Southeast Asia, as well as Western converts who trained in Asia, have played a crucial role in transmitting the teachings. They have established meditation centers, conducted retreats, and offered teachings that resonate with Western audiences. These efforts have contributed to the development of a vibrant Theravada community in the West.

One of the key factors driving the interest in Theravada Buddhism in the West is the appeal of mindfulness and meditation practices. These practices have been embraced by individuals seeking stress reduction, emotional well-being, and spiritual insight. Mindfulness has found its way into various sectors, including healthcare, education, and corporate settings, where it is valued for its practical benefits. The secular application of mindfulness has introduced many to the principles of Theravada Buddhism.

The adaptation of Theravada teachings to Western contexts has involved a process of cultural translation and reinterpretation. Western practitioners have engaged with the teachings in ways that address contemporary concerns and values, such as individualism, scientific inquiry, and social justice. This process has led to new interpretations and expressions of Theravada Buddhism, reflecting the diverse backgrounds and experiences of Western practitioners.

As Theravada Buddhism continues to grow in the West, it faces both opportunities and challenges. The tradition's emphasis on meditation and mindfulness offers a valuable resource for individuals seeking meaning and connection in an increasingly complex world. However, the adaptation of the teachings to Western contexts requires careful consideration to ensure that the core principles and values are preserved. Through dialogue, exploration, and mutual respect, Theravada Buddhism continues to find its place in the Western spiritual landscape, offering a path to insight, compassion, and inner peace.

CORE TEACHINGS AND DOCTRINES

THE FOUR NOBLE TRUTHS

The Four Noble Truths are the cornerstone of the Buddha's teachings, providing a framework for understanding the nature of suffering and the path to liberation. The First Noble Truth is the truth of dukkha, often translated as "suffering" or "unsatisfactoriness." This truth acknowledges that life is filled with various forms of suffering, such as pain, loss, and disappointment. The Buddha taught that recognizing the presence of suffering is the first step toward addressing it.

The Second Noble Truth identifies the cause of suffering as tanha, or "craving." This craving arises from our desire for pleasure, existence, and non-existence. It leads to attachment and clinging, which perpetuate the cycle of suffering. The Buddha emphasized that understanding the nature of craving and its role in our lives is essential for breaking free from its grip. By examining our desires and attachments, we can begin to uncover the root causes of our suffering.

The Third Noble Truth offers hope by affirming the possibility of the cessation of suffering. This truth states that it is possible to overcome craving and attachment, leading to the end of suffering. The Buddha called this state nibbana, or "liberation." Nibbana represents the ultimate freedom from the cycle of birth, death, and rebirth, as well as the cessation of mental and emotional turmoil. It is a state of peace, clarity, and contentment.

The Fourth Noble Truth outlines the path to the cessation of suffering, known as the Noble Eightfold Path. This path is a comprehensive guide to ethical conduct, mental discipline, and wisdom. It provides practical steps for transforming our lives and cultivating the qualities necessary for achieving liberation. The Buddha taught that by following this path, individuals can gradually overcome ignorance and craving, leading to the realization of nibbana.

Together, the Four Noble Truths form the foundation of the Buddha's teachings. They offer a practical and profound approach to understanding and addressing the challenges of human existence. By recognizing the nature of suffering, understanding its causes, and following the path to liberation, individuals can embark on a transformative journey toward peace and fulfillment. The Four Noble Truths continue to inspire and guide countless individuals on their spiritual paths.

THE NOBLE EIGHTFOLD PATH

The Noble Eightfold Path is the Buddha's blueprint for living a life that leads to the cessation of suffering and the realization of enlightenment. It is divided into three main categories: wisdom, ethical conduct, and mental discipline. Each category encompasses specific practices that contribute to personal growth and transformation. The path is not a linear progression but rather an interconnected set of practices that support and reinforce one another.

The first category, wisdom, includes Right Understanding and Right Intention. Right Understanding involves seeing things as they truly are, recognizing the nature of suffering, and understanding the principles of karma and rebirth. Right Intention involves cultivating a mindset of renunciation, goodwill, and harmlessness. These two aspects of wisdom lay the foundation for ethical conduct and mental discipline.

The second category, ethical conduct, consists of Right Speech, Right Action, and Right Livelihood. Right Speech involves speaking truthfully, kindly, and constructively, avoiding lies, gossip, and harmful words. Right Action entails behaving ethically and compassionately and refraining from actions that cause harm to others. Right Livelihood involves choosing an occupation that is ethical and does not contribute to suffering or exploitation.

The third category, mental discipline, includes Right Effort, Right Mindfulness, and Right Concentration. Right Effort involves cultivating positive mental states and preventing unwholesome ones. Right Mindfulness is the practice of being present and aware in each moment, observing thoughts, feelings, and sensations without attachment or aversion. Right Concentration involves developing deep focus and concentration through meditation, leading to states of profound calm and insight.

The Noble Eightfold Path is a holistic approach to spiritual practice that encompasses all aspects of life. It provides a practical guide for cultivating wisdom, compassion, and mental clarity, ultimately leading to liberation. By following this path, individuals can transform their minds and hearts, creating the conditions for lasting peace and fulfillment. The path is accessible to everyone, offering a timeless and universal framework for personal growth and spiritual awakening.

THE THREE MARKS OF EXISTENCE

The Three Marks of Existence are fundamental insights into the nature of reality that form the basis of the Buddha's teachings. They are impermanence (anicca), suffering (dukkha), and non-self (anatta). Understanding these marks is essential for developing a deeper awareness of the true nature of life and for progressing on the path to liberation. These insights challenge our habitual perceptions and encourage us to see beyond the surface of our experiences.

Impermanence, or anicca, refers to the constant change and flux that characterizes all aspects of existence. Nothing in life is permanent; everything is in a state of constant transformation. This insight helps us recognize that clinging to things, people, or experiences leads to suffering, as they are all subject to change and loss. By accepting impermanence, we can cultivate a more flexible and resilient approach to life, reducing our attachment to fleeting pleasures and conditions.

Suffering, or dukkha, is the pervasive unsatisfactoriness and discomfort that accompany human existence. It encompasses not only the obvious forms of suffering, such as pain and loss but also the subtle dissatisfaction that arises from the impermanent nature of life. The Buddha taught that understanding the reality of dukkha is essential for developing compassion and empathy for ourselves and others. By acknowledging the presence of suffering, we can begin to address its causes and cultivate a more peaceful and contented mind.

Non-self, or anatta, is the insight that there is no permanent, unchanging self or soul. The belief in a fixed, independent self is a source of attachment and suffering, as it leads to the desire to protect and preserve this self. The Buddha taught that what we consider to be "self" is actually a collection of changing physical and mental processes. By recognizing the illusory nature of the self, we can loosen our attachment to ego and identity, opening the door to greater freedom and liberation.

The Three Marks of Existence provide a profound perspective on the nature of reality, challenging our habitual ways of seeing and relating to the world. By contemplating these insights, we can develop a deeper understanding of the causes of suffering and the path to liberation. These teachings encourage us to let go of attachment and aversion, cultivating a more open and accepting attitude toward the changing nature of life. In doing so, we can experience greater peace, clarity, and freedom.

DEPENDENT ORIGINATION

Dependent Origination, or paticca-samuppada, is a central concept in the Buddha's teachings that explains the interconnectedness and interdependence of all phenomena. It describes the process by which suffering arises and the conditions necessary for its cessation. Dependent Origination reveals that nothing exists in isolation; everything arises in dependence on multiple causes and conditions. This insight challenges the notion of independent existence and emphasizes the complexity and interconnectedness of life.

The formula of Dependent Origination consists of twelve links, each representing a stage in the cycle of existence. It begins with ignorance (avijja), which gives rise to volitional formations (sankhara), leading to consciousness (viññana), and so on, culminating in the experience of birth, aging, and death. Each link in the chain conditions the next, illustrating how suffering arises from a web of interconnected causes and conditions.

Ignorance, as the starting point of the chain, is the fundamental misunderstanding of the nature of reality. It is the failure to see the Three Marks of Existence and the true nature of the self. This ignorance leads to the formation of desires, attachments, and actions that perpetuate the cycle of suffering. By understanding and addressing ignorance, we can begin to unravel the chain of Dependent Origination and move toward liberation.

Dependent Origination also highlights the possibility of breaking the cycle of suffering. By identifying the conditions that give rise to suffering, we can work to eliminate them, creating the conditions for liberation. This process involves cultivating wisdom, ethical conduct, and mindfulness, which help to counteract ignorance and attachment. Through this practice, we can gradually dismantle the causes of suffering and experience greater freedom and peace.

The teaching of Dependent Origination offers a profound understanding of the nature of reality and the dynamics of suffering. It encourages us to see beyond the surface of our experiences and recognize the interconnectedness of all phenomena. By understanding the conditions that give rise to suffering, we can take steps to transform our lives and move toward liberation. This insight provides a powerful framework for personal growth and spiritual awakening, offering a path to lasting peace and fulfillment.

KARMA AND REBIRTH

Karma and rebirth are central concepts in Buddhist philosophy that explain the moral and ethical dimensions of existence. Karma refers to the actions and intentions that shape our experiences and influence our future. It is not merely a system of rewards and punishments but rather a natural law of cause and effect. The Buddha taught that our actions, whether positive or negative, have consequences that affect our present and future circumstances.

Karma operates on the principle that every action has an intention behind it, and this intention determines the karmic outcome. Positive intentions lead to positive outcomes, while negative intentions result in negative outcomes. This understanding emphasizes the importance of cultivating wholesome intentions and actions as they contribute to a more peaceful and fulfilling life. The Buddha encouraged individuals to take responsibility for their actions and to make ethical choices that promote well-being for themselves and others.

Rebirth, or samsara, refers to the cycle of birth, death, and rebirth that continues until liberation is attained. According to Buddhist teachings, the nature of our rebirth is determined by our accumulated karma. The cycle of rebirth is not limited to a single lifetime but spans countless lifetimes, with each life offering an opportunity for growth and transformation. The ultimate goal is to break free from this cycle and attain nibbana, or liberation.

The concepts of karma and rebirth underscore the interconnectedness of all life and the continuity of consciousness beyond a single lifetime. They encourage individuals to consider the long-term consequences of their actions and to live in a way that promotes positive karma. By cultivating compassion, wisdom, and ethical conduct, individuals can influence their future experiences and progress on the path to liberation.

Karma and rebirth also offer a framework for understanding the diversity of human experiences. They explain why individuals may face different challenges and opportunities, emphasizing the role of past actions in shaping present circumstances. This understanding fosters a sense of empathy and compassion, as we recognize that each person's journey is shaped by their unique karma. By acknowledging the complexity of karma and rebirth, we can cultivate a more compassionate and understanding perspective on life.

THE CONCEPT OF NIBBANA (NIRVANA)

Nibbana, or Nirvana, is the ultimate goal of Buddhist practice, representing the cessation of suffering and the attainment of liberation. It is a state of profound peace, clarity, and freedom from the cycle of birth and death. Nibbana is not a place or a heavenly realm but rather a transformation of consciousness, a complete release from ignorance, craving, and attachment. It is the realization of the true nature of reality and the end of the cycle of samsara.

The Buddha described Nibbana as the highest happiness, beyond the pleasures and pains of worldly existence. It is a state of perfect equanimity and contentment, free from the turmoil and distractions of the mind. Nibbana is characterized by the absence of greed, hatred, and delusion, the three poisons that fuel the cycle of suffering. By overcoming these defilements, individuals can experience the peace and freedom of Nibbana.

Achieving Nibbana requires dedicated practice and the cultivation of wisdom, ethical conduct, and mental discipline. The Noble Eightfold Path provides a framework for developing the qualities necessary for liberation. Through meditation, mindfulness, and the practice of compassion, individuals can gradually transform their minds and hearts, creating the conditions for the realization of Nibbana. The journey to Nibbana is a personal and transformative process, requiring patience, perseverance, and dedication.

Nibbana is often described as the "unconditioned" or "unborn," highlighting its transcendence of the conditions and limitations of worldly existence. It is a state beyond duality and conceptual understanding, experienced directly through insight and realization. The Buddha emphasized that Nibbana is accessible to all individuals, regardless of their background or circumstances. It is a universal and timeless truth, offering a path to liberation for anyone willing to undertake the journey.

The concept of Nibbana provides a vision of human potential and the possibility of transformation. It offers a path to freedom from suffering and a deeper understanding of the nature of reality. By aspiring to attain Nibbana, individuals are inspired to live with greater compassion, wisdom, and integrity, contributing to a more peaceful and harmonious world. The pursuit of Nibbana is a journey of self-discovery and spiritual awakening, offering the promise of liberation and the realization of our true nature.

THE FIVE AGGREGATES (SKANDHAS)

The Five Aggregates, or Skandhas, are a fundamental concept in Buddhist philosophy that describe the components of human existence. They provide a framework for understanding the nature of the self and the processes that give rise to the experience of being. The Five Aggregates are form (rupa), feeling (vedana), perception (sanna), mental formations (sankhara), and consciousness (viññana). Together, they constitute the totality of human experience.

Form, or rupa, refers to the physical body and the material world. It encompasses the elements and conditions that give rise to our physical existence. The Buddha taught that form is impermanent and subject to change, reminding us of the transient nature of our physical bodies. By recognizing the impermanence of form, we can cultivate a more balanced and detached relationship with our bodies and the material world.

Feeling, or vedana, is the sensory experience of pleasure, pain, or neutrality that arises from contact with the world. Feelings are the immediate responses to sensory input, influencing our thoughts and actions. The Buddha emphasized the importance of mindfulness in observing feelings, allowing us to respond skillfully rather than react impulsively. By understanding the nature of feelings, we can develop greater equanimity and reduce our attachment to fleeting pleasures and discomforts.

Perception, or sanna, involves the recognition and interpretation of sensory input. It is the process by which we categorize and make sense of our experiences. Perception shapes our understanding of the world and influences our beliefs and attitudes. The Buddha taught that perception is conditioned by past experiences and mental habits, highlighting the importance of cultivating awareness and discernment in our perceptions.

Mental formations, or sankhara, refer to the mental states, intentions, and attitudes that shape our actions and experiences. They include emotions, thoughts, and volitions, which influence our behavior and contribute to the formation of karma. The Buddha encouraged the cultivation of positive mental formations, such as loving-kindness, compassion, and generosity, to counteract negative tendencies and promote well-being.

Consciousness, or viññana, is the awareness of sensory and mental phenomena. It is the faculty that allows us to experience and interact with the world. Consciousness is not a fixed or permanent entity but a dynamic process that arises in dependence on the other aggregates. The Buddha taught that consciousness is conditioned and interdependent, challenging the notion of a fixed, independent self. By understanding the nature of consciousness, we can develop insight into the interconnectedness of all aspects of experience.

The Five Aggregates provide a comprehensive framework for understanding the nature of the self and the processes that contribute to the experience of being. They challenge the notion of a fixed, independent self, highlighting the interdependent and dynamic nature of human existence. By contemplating the aggregates, we can develop a deeper understanding of the causes of suffering and the path to liberation, cultivating insight, compassion, and wisdom on our spiritual journey.

THE PALI CANON

VINAYA PITAKA

The Vinaya Pitaka is one of the three major sections of the Pali Canon, and it holds the rules and regulations for Buddhist monastic life. These rules are essential for maintaining discipline among monks and nuns, ensuring they live harmoniously and support their spiritual practice. The Vinaya Pitaka covers a wide range of topics, from the proper way to wear robes to the appropriate interactions with laypeople. These guidelines were established by the Buddha to create a conducive environment for spiritual growth and communal living.

At its core, the Vinaya Pitaka is about fostering a life of simplicity and detachment from worldly concerns. Monks and nuns are expected to live with minimal possessions, which helps them focus on their spiritual goals. The rules promote virtues like humility, honesty, and self-restraint, which are essential for the spiritual path. By adhering to the

Vinaya, monastics create a supportive community that exemplifies the teachings of the Buddha and inspires lay followers to cultivate similar virtues.

The Vinaya Pitaka also addresses how to handle various situations and conflicts that might arise in monastic life. This includes procedures for resolving disputes, administering disciplinary actions, and ensuring the well-being of the community. These regulations help prevent misunderstandings and maintain harmony within the Sangha, allowing monastics to focus on their practice without unnecessary distractions. The rules also evolve over time, reflecting the changing needs and contexts of the monastic community.

Studying the Vinaya Pitaka provides valuable insights into the daily lives of monastics and the challenges they face. It offers a glimpse into the historical context of the Buddha's time, showing how he adapted his teachings to address specific issues. For lay practitioners, understanding the Vinaya can deepen their appreciation of the monastic lifestyle and the commitment required to follow the path. It also underscores the importance of discipline and ethical conduct in the broader Buddhist tradition.

The Vinaya Pitaka continues to be relevant today, guiding monastics in their pursuit of enlightenment. It serves as a reminder of the importance of discipline and ethical behavior in spiritual practice. By upholding these principles, monastics set an example for laypeople, demonstrating that a life of simplicity and integrity is essential for realizing the Buddha's teachings. The Vinaya Pitaka remains a vital part of the Pali Canon, providing a foundation for the monastic community and its role in preserving and transmitting the Dharma.

SUTTA PITAKA

The Sutta Pitaka is a vast collection of the Buddha's discourses and teachings, forming the heart of the Pali Canon. These texts cover a wide range of topics, from ethical guidelines and meditation practices to profound philosophical insights. The Sutta Pitaka is divided into several collections, known as Nikayas, each with its unique focus and style. The discourses offer practical advice for living a life aligned with the Buddha's teachings, providing a roadmap for spiritual growth and liberation.

The Sutta Pitaka contains some of the most well-known teachings of the Buddha, including the Four Noble Truths and the Noble Eightfold Path. These core principles form the foundation of Buddhist practice, guiding individuals toward wisdom, ethical conduct, and mental discipline. The discourses also address everyday challenges, offering guidance on relationships, work, and personal development. The Sutta Pitaka's teachings are accessible and relevant, providing timeless wisdom for navigating the complexities of life.

One of the unique features of the Sutta Pitaka is its emphasis on storytelling and dialogue. The Buddha often used stories and analogies to convey complex ideas in an engaging and relatable way. These narratives capture the imagination and inspire reflection, allowing listeners to connect with the teachings on a deeper level. The Sutta Pitaka's storytelling tradition continues to resonate with modern audiences, highlighting the universal themes and truths that transcend time and culture.

The Sutta Pitaka also emphasizes the importance of direct experience and personal insight. The Buddha encouraged his followers to question, investigate, and verify his teachings through their own experience. This approach fosters a spirit of inquiry and critical thinking, empowering individuals to take responsibility for their spiritual journey. The Sutta Pitaka's teachings are not dogmatic but rather an invitation to explore and discover the truth for oneself.

The Sutta Pitaka remains a vital source of inspiration and guidance for Buddhists worldwide. Its teachings offer practical wisdom for cultivating a life of mindfulness, compassion, and understanding. By engaging with the discourses, individuals can deepen their understanding of the Buddha's teachings and apply them to their lives. The Sutta Pitaka continues to be a rich and diverse resource for those seeking to embark on a path of spiritual awakening and transformation.

ABHIDHAMMA PITAKA

The Abhidhamma Pitaka is the third major section of the Pali Canon, offering a detailed and systematic analysis of the Buddha's teachings. Unlike the Sutta Pitaka, which presents the teachings in narrative form, the Abhidhamma provides a theoretical framework for understanding the mind and reality. It breaks down complex psychological and philosophical concepts into precise categories and classifications, offering insights into the nature of consciousness and mental processes.

At its core, the Abhidhamma Pitaka explores the workings of the mind, examining how thoughts, emotions, and perceptions arise and interact. It identifies distinct mental factors and processes, analyzing their role in shaping our experience. This in-depth exploration of the mind provides a foundation for developing mindfulness and insight, enabling practitioners to recognize and transform unwholesome mental states. The Abhidhamma's teachings offer a roadmap for cultivating a clear and focused mind.

The Abhidhamma Pitaka also delves into the nature of reality, examining the interplay between mind and matter. It explores the concept of dependent origination, which describes how phenomena arise in dependence on various causes and conditions. This understanding challenges the notion of a fixed, independent self, highlighting the interconnected and impermanent nature of existence. The Abhidhamma's teachings encourage practitioners to develop a deeper awareness of the true nature of reality.

For those interested in advanced Buddhist studies, the Abhidhamma Pitaka offers a rich and complex body of knowledge. It provides a comprehensive framework for understanding the intricacies of the mind and the nature of reality. Scholars and practitioners can engage with the Abhidhamma to deepen their understanding of the Buddha's teachings and their practical applications. The Abhidhamma Pitaka serves as a valuable resource for those seeking to explore the deeper dimensions of Buddhist philosophy and psychology.

While the Abhidhamma Pitaka may appear abstract and theoretical, its teachings have practical implications for daily life and meditation practice. By understanding the nature of the mind and its processes, practitioners can cultivate greater mindfulness, clarity, and insight. The Abhidhamma's teachings offer a path to personal transformation, helping individuals develop the qualities necessary for achieving liberation. For those willing to engage with its complexities, the Abhidhamma Pitaka provides a profound and transformative perspective on the Buddhist path.

COMPILATION AND PRESERVATION

The compilation and preservation of the Pali Canon are remarkable achievements that have ensured the survival of the Buddha's teachings for over two millennia. After the Buddha's passing, his disciples faced the challenge of preserving his teachings in a rapidly changing world. The first Buddhist council was convened to compile the teachings, with Ananda reciting the Sutta Pitaka and Upali reciting the Vinaya Pitaka. This oral tradition ensured the accuracy and integrity of the teachings before they were eventually written down.

The decision to commit the Pali Canon to writing was a significant milestone in Buddhist history. The texts were first written down in Sri Lanka during the first century BCE in response to concerns about the loss of the oral tradition due to social and political upheavals. The written compilation of the Pali Canon was a monumental effort involving the collaboration of numerous scholars and scribes. This endeavor ensured that the teachings would be preserved for future generations.

The preservation of the Pali Canon has been a continuous effort, with monastic communities playing a crucial role in its transmission. Monasteries served as centers of learning and scholarship, where monks memorized, studied, and taught the texts. The dedication and discipline of these monastic communities have ensured the survival of the Pali

Canon, allowing it to be passed down through generations. Their efforts have preserved the teachings' authenticity and integrity, providing a reliable source of guidance for practitioners.

Throughout history, the Pali Canon has faced challenges, including invasions, natural disasters, and cultural shifts. Yet, the resilience and commitment of the Buddhist community have ensured its continued survival. The texts have been translated into various languages, making them accessible to a global audience. Modern technology has further facilitated the preservation and dissemination of the Pali Canon, allowing it to reach new audiences and inspire a diverse range of practitioners.

The compilation and preservation of the Pali Canon are a testament to the enduring power and relevance of the Buddha's teachings. They provide a foundation for the study and practice of Buddhism, offering a rich and diverse body of knowledge for those seeking to understand the Dharma. The Pali Canon continues to be a source of inspiration and guidance, shaping the spiritual journey of countless individuals across the world.

KEY TEXTS AND COMMENTARIES

The Pali Canon is home to a wealth of key texts and commentaries that have shaped the understanding and practice of Buddhism. Among the most influential texts are the Dhammapada, the Majjhima Nikaya, and the Visuddhimagga, each offering unique insights into the Buddha's teachings. These texts provide practical guidance, philosophical exploration, and meditative instructions, serving as invaluable resources for practitioners and scholars alike.

The Dhammapada is one of the most widely read and cherished texts in the Pali Canon. It is a collection of verses that encapsulate the core teachings of the Buddha, offering practical wisdom for everyday life. The Dhammapada's concise and memorable verses cover topics such as mindfulness, compassion, and ethical conduct, making it an accessible and inspiring guide for those seeking to cultivate a life of virtue and wisdom.

The Majjhima Nikaya is a collection of middle-length discourses that delve into various aspects of the Buddha's teachings. These discourses address a wide range of topics, from meditation practices and ethical guidelines to profound philosophical inquiries. The Majjhima Nikaya's teachings offer a comprehensive exploration of the Dharma, providing a roadmap for personal and spiritual development. Its discourses continue to inspire and guide practitioners on their journey.

The Visuddhimagga, or "Path of Purification," is a comprehensive manual of meditation and ethical practice written by the Buddhist scholar Buddhaghosa in the 5th century CE. It is considered one of the most important commentaries on the Pali Canon, offering detailed instructions on meditation techniques and ethical conduct. The Visuddhimagga provides a systematic and detailed guide to the path of purification, emphasizing the development of morality, concentration, and wisdom.

Commentaries play a vital role in interpreting and elucidating the teachings of the Pali Canon. These texts, written by esteemed Buddhist scholars and teachers, offer insights and explanations that deepen our understanding of the Dharma. Commentaries provide context, clarify complex concepts, and explore the nuances of the teachings, enriching our study and practice. They serve as a bridge between the ancient texts and contemporary practitioners, ensuring the teachings remain relevant and accessible.

Key texts and commentaries continue to be essential resources for those seeking to explore the depths of the Buddha's teachings. They offer a wealth of knowledge and guidance, inspiring individuals to cultivate a life of mindfulness, compassion, and wisdom. By engaging with these texts, practitioners can deepen their understanding of the Dharma and apply its principles to their lives. The key texts and commentaries of the Pali Canon remain a rich and diverse treasure trove of wisdom for the spiritual journey.

LANGUAGE AND STYLE

The Pali Canon is written in the Pali language, an ancient Indo-Aryan language closely related to Sanskrit. Pali is considered the canonical language of Theravada Buddhism and is used to preserve the teachings of the Buddha. The language and style of the Pali Canon reflect the oral tradition from which it originated, with a focus on clarity, memorability, and accessibility. The texts are composed in a straightforward and direct style, making them accessible to a wide range of audiences.

The Pali language is characterized by its simplicity and precision, allowing the teachings to be conveyed clearly and effectively. This simplicity is reflected in the use of repetitive structures, mnemonic devices, and lists, which aid in memorization and recall. The repetitive style of the Pali Canon ensures that key teachings and concepts are reinforced, facilitating their transmission and understanding. The language's clarity and structure enable practitioners to engage with the teachings meaningfully.

The style of the Pali Canon emphasizes the use of analogies, similes, and stories to convey complex ideas. These literary devices capture the imagination and make abstract concepts more relatable and understandable. The Buddha often used everyday examples and vivid imagery to illustrate his teachings, allowing listeners to connect with the teachings personally. This approach ensures the teachings remain relevant and engaging, resonating with audiences across time and culture.

The Pali Canon's language and style have been preserved and transmitted through various translations and adaptations. While the original Pali texts remain the authoritative source of the teachings, translations into other languages have made the teachings accessible to a global audience. These translations strive to capture the essence and meaning of the original texts while ensuring they are understandable and relevant to contemporary practitioners.

The language and style of the Pali Canon continue to inspire and guide individuals on their spiritual journey. They offer a timeless and universal expression of the Buddha's teachings, providing a foundation for study, reflection, and practice. By engaging with the language and style of the Pali Canon, practitioners can deepen their connection to the teachings and apply their wisdom to their lives. The Pali Canon's language and style remain a vital and vibrant expression of the Dharma, offering a path to insight and liberation.

IMPORTANCE IN DAILY PRACTICE

The Pali Canon holds a central place in the daily practice of Buddhists, offering guidance and inspiration for living a life aligned with the Buddha's teachings. Its teachings provide practical tools for cultivating mindfulness, ethical conduct, and wisdom, supporting individuals on their spiritual journey. By engaging with the Pali Canon, practitioners can deepen their understanding of the Dharma and apply its principles to their everyday lives.

One of the key aspects of the Pali Canon's importance in daily practice is its emphasis on mindfulness and meditation. The teachings encourage individuals to develop awareness and presence in each moment, fostering a deeper connection to their thoughts, feelings, and actions. By cultivating mindfulness, practitioners can develop greater insight into the nature of their mind and the causes of suffering, enabling them to respond to life's challenges with clarity and compassion.

The Pali Canon also emphasizes the importance of ethical conduct, offering guidelines for living a life of integrity and virtue. The teachings encourage individuals to cultivate positive qualities such as kindness, generosity, and patience while avoiding harmful actions and intentions. By adhering to ethical principles, practitioners create a foundation for personal and spiritual growth, fostering a sense of peace and well-being in themselves and others.

The Pali Canon's teachings on wisdom and insight are essential for deepening one's understanding of the nature of reality and the path to liberation. The texts provide guidance on developing discernment and understanding, encouraging individuals to question and investigate the nature of their experience. By cultivating wisdom, practitioners can overcome ignorance and delusion, leading to a greater sense of freedom and liberation.

Engaging with the Pali Canon in daily practice offers a path to personal transformation and spiritual awakening. The teachings provide a roadmap for cultivating the qualities necessary for achieving liberation, offering guidance and inspiration for living a life of mindfulness, compassion, and wisdom. By integrating the teachings of the Pali Canon into their lives, practitioners can experience greater peace, clarity, and fulfillment on their spiritual journey.

MONASTIC LIFE AND THE SANGHA

ORDINATION PROCESS

The journey to becoming a Buddhist monk or nun begins with the ordination process, a rite of passage that marks the transition from lay life to monastic life. This process involves several steps, starting with seeking permission from one's family. Once a family gives its blessing, the aspiring monastic must find a teacher or mentor within the monastic community who will act as a guide through the ordination process and beyond. This mentor helps them understand the responsibilities and commitments involved in monastic life.

The initial stage of ordination is known as pabbajja, or the novice ordination. During this ceremony, the novice shaves their head and dons the monastic robes, symbolizing their renunciation of worldly life. They take a set of ten precepts, which include rules against killing, stealing, and lying. This stage is a time for learning and adaptation, where the novice lives in the monastery and observes the daily routine of the monks and nuns, absorbing the discipline and practices of monastic life.

After a period as a novice, which can last several years, the individual may seek full ordination, or upasampada. This ceremony is more formal and involves the presence of a quorum of senior monks. The candidate must demonstrate their commitment to the monastic life and their understanding of the rules and teachings. Full ordination requires the acceptance of the full set of monastic precepts, which are more extensive than those of a novice. This commitment is not taken lightly, as it signifies a lifelong dedication to the monastic path.

During the ordination ceremony, the new monk or nun receives a new name, marking their new identity as a member of the Sangha, the Buddhist monastic community. This name is often chosen to reflect qualities or virtues that the individual aspires to cultivate. The ceremony is a joyous occasion, often attended by the local lay community, who offer support and encouragement to the new monastic. This public recognition reinforces the connection between the monastic and lay communities.

The ordination process is both a personal and communal journey. For the individual, it represents a profound commitment to spiritual practice and a renunciation of worldly attachments. For the monastic community, each new ordination strengthens the Sangha and renews its mission to preserve and transmit the teachings of the Buddha. This tradition of ordination has been carried on for centuries, maintaining the continuity and integrity of the Buddhist monastic tradition.

DAILY ROUTINE OF MONKS AND NUNS

The daily routine of monks and nuns is structured around the principles of discipline, mindfulness, and simplicity. Each day begins early, often before sunrise, with meditation and chanting. These morning practices help to cultivate mindfulness and set a positive tone for the day. Meditation is a cornerstone of monastic life, allowing monks and nuns to develop focus, concentration, and insight. The chanting of Buddhist texts reinforces the teachings and fosters a sense of community and shared purpose.

After morning meditation, monks and nuns typically engage in communal activities, such as cleaning and maintaining the monastery. This work is done mindfully, transforming routine tasks into opportunities for practice. Monastics are taught to approach every task, no matter how mundane, with full attention and presence. This practice of mindfulness in daily activities helps to cultivate a sense of inner peace and contentment, reinforcing the values of simplicity and detachment.

The mid-morning meal is another important part of the monastic routine. Monks and nuns eat only what is offered by lay supporters, practicing the principle of dana, or generosity. This dependence on the lay community fosters humility and gratitude, reminding monastics of the interconnectedness of all beings. Meals are often eaten in silence, allowing for reflection and appreciation. This practice of mindful eating encourages an awareness of the present moment and a deepened connection to the body and mind.

The afternoon is typically devoted to study, teaching, and individual meditation practice. Monks and nuns study Buddhist texts, reflecting on the teachings and discussing them with their peers. They may also lead meditation sessions or give teachings to lay practitioners, sharing their insights and experiences. This balance of study, teaching, and practice helps to deepen their understanding of the Dharma and strengthens their commitment to the monastic path.

Evening meditation and chanting bring the day to a close, providing a time for reflection and introspection. These practices help monks and nuns to let go of the day's distractions and cultivate a sense of inner peace before sleep. The daily routine of monastics is designed to support their spiritual development, fostering discipline, mindfulness, and compassion. By living a life of simplicity and focus, monks and nuns embody the teachings of the Buddha and inspire others to follow the path of awakening.

MONASTIC RULES AND DISCIPLINE

Monastic rules and discipline are central to the life of monks and nuns, providing a framework for ethical conduct and spiritual development. These rules, known as the Vinaya, govern every aspect of monastic life, from daily routines to interactions with others. The Vinaya is designed to create a harmonious and supportive environment that fosters mindfulness, self-discipline, and detachment from worldly attachments. Adhering to these rules helps monks and nuns cultivate the virtues necessary for spiritual growth.

The Vinaya includes a comprehensive set of precepts that guide the behavior of monastics. These precepts cover a wide range of topics, including celibacy, honesty, and non-harming. Monastics are expected to live simply, owning only a few possessions and relying on the generosity of the lay community for their basic needs. This lifestyle encourages detachment from material wealth and fosters a spirit of contentment and gratitude.

The rules also emphasize the importance of community and harmony within the Sangha. Monastics are encouraged to support and respect one another, fostering an atmosphere of mutual understanding and cooperation. Disputes and conflicts are addressed through established procedures, ensuring that they are resolved fairly and peacefully. This emphasis on community and cooperation helps to create a supportive environment for spiritual practice and growth.

Discipline is a key aspect of monastic life, requiring a commitment to self-control and mindfulness. Monks and nuns are expected to follow a strict daily routine, maintaining focus and dedication to their practice. This discipline extends to thoughts, speech, and actions, encouraging monastics to cultivate positive mental states and avoid harmful behaviors. By adhering to these rules, monastics develop the qualities of patience, perseverance, and equanimity, which are essential for the path to awakening.

While the Vinaya provides a structured framework for monastic life, it is not a rigid or dogmatic system. The rules are designed to be flexible and adaptable, allowing for interpretation and modification in response to changing circumstances. This adaptability ensures that the Vinaya remains relevant and applicable to contemporary monastic life, preserving the integrity and continuity of the Buddhist monastic tradition.

ROLE OF THE SANGHA IN THE COMMUNITY

The Sangha, or monastic community, plays a vital role in the broader Buddhist community, serving as a source of spiritual guidance, support, and inspiration. Monks and nuns are seen as living embodiments of the Buddha's teachings, providing an example of ethical conduct, mindfulness, and compassion. Their presence in the community offers a tangible connection to the Dharma, inspiring laypeople to cultivate similar virtues in their own lives.

One of the primary roles of the Sangha is to preserve and transmit the teachings of the Buddha. Monks and nuns dedicate their lives to studying and practicing the Dharma, ensuring its continuity and relevance. They serve as teachers and mentors, offering guidance and support to those seeking to deepen their understanding of the teachings. Through their example and instruction, the Sangha helps to nurture and sustain the spiritual growth of the community.

The Sangha also plays a crucial role in the performance of rituals and ceremonies, providing a focal point for communal practice and devotion. Monks and nuns lead chanting, meditation, and other practices, creating opportunities for laypeople to engage with the teachings and strengthen their connection to the Dharma. These communal activities foster a sense of unity and shared purpose, reinforcing the bonds between the monastic and lay communities.

In addition to their spiritual role, the Sangha often serves as a center of social and cultural life within the community. Monasteries and temples provide a gathering place for festivals, celebrations, and other events, bringing people together and fostering a sense of belonging and community. The Sangha's presence and participation in these activities help to promote social cohesion and mutual support, contributing to the well-being and resilience of the community.

The relationship between the Sangha and the lay community is one of mutual respect and interdependence. Laypeople provide material support to the monastic community, offering food, clothing, and other necessities. In return, monks and nuns offer spiritual guidance and teachings, sharing their insights and experiences with the lay community. This reciprocal relationship strengthens the bonds between monastics and laypeople, creating a supportive and interconnected community that embodies the principles of the Dharma.

MONASTIC EDUCATION AND TRAINING

Monastic education and training are essential components of the Buddhist monastic tradition, providing the knowledge and skills necessary for spiritual growth and understanding. The education of monks and nuns begins with the study of the Pali Canon, the foundational texts of Theravada Buddhism. These texts cover a wide range of topics, from ethical guidelines and meditation practices to philosophical teachings and historical accounts. Mastery of these texts is crucial for deepening one's understanding of the Dharma and for fulfilling the role of teacher and mentor within the community.

In addition to studying the Pali Canon, monastics engage in the practice of meditation, developing the skills of mindfulness, concentration, and insight. Meditation is a cornerstone of monastic life, providing a direct experience of the teachings and fostering the development of wisdom and compassion. Monks and nuns are trained in various meditation techniques, allowing them to cultivate a focused and disciplined mind. This practice is essential for personal growth and for serving as a guide and example to others.

Monastic training also emphasizes the cultivation of ethical conduct and moral integrity. Monks and nuns are expected to adhere to the Vinaya, the code of monastic discipline, which governs their behavior and interactions with others. This training fosters the development of virtues such as honesty, humility, and self-restraint, essential for living a life of simplicity and renunciation. By embodying these qualities, monastics serve as role models for the lay community and inspire others to cultivate similar virtues.

Mentorship and guidance from senior monks and nuns play a crucial role in the education and training of monastics. Experienced teachers provide instruction, support, and encouragement, helping novices navigate the challenges of monastic life. This mentorship fosters a sense of community and continuity within the Sangha, ensuring the transmission of knowledge and experience from one generation to the next. The relationships between mentors and mentees are characterized by mutual respect and trust, providing a supportive environment for personal and spiritual growth.

The education and training of monks and nuns are ongoing processes, with continued study and practice throughout their monastic lives. Monastics are encouraged to deepen their understanding of the teachings and to engage in self-reflection and introspection. This lifelong commitment to learning and growth ensures that the Sangha remains a vibrant and dynamic force within the Buddhist community, capable of responding to the needs and challenges of contemporary life while preserving the integrity and continuity of the tradition.

LAY SUPPORT AND DANA (GENEROSITY)

Lay support and the practice of dana, or generosity, are essential elements of the relationship between the monastic and lay communities. Dana is a fundamental principle in Buddhism, emphasizing the importance of giving and sharing as expressions of compassion and interconnectedness. Laypeople support the monastic community by providing material necessities, such as food, clothing, and medicine, allowing monks and nuns to focus on their spiritual practices and teachings.

The practice of dana fosters a sense of mutual respect and interdependence between monastics and laypeople. By offering material support to the Sangha, laypeople participate in the preservation and transmission of the Dharma, contributing to the well-being and resilience of the Buddhist community. This practice of generosity is seen as a virtuous act that benefits both the giver and the recipient, cultivating positive karma and reinforcing the bonds of community and connection.

In return for their support, laypeople receive spiritual guidance and teachings from the monastic community. Monks and nuns offer instruction, encouragement, and insight, helping lay practitioners deepen their understanding of the Dharma and apply its principles to their lives. This reciprocal relationship strengthens the spiritual growth of both monastics and laypeople, fostering a sense of shared purpose and commitment to the path of awakening.

The practice of dana also extends beyond the material realm, encompassing acts of kindness, compassion, and service. Laypeople are encouraged to cultivate generosity in all aspects of their lives, developing qualities such as empathy, understanding, and patience. This broader interpretation of dana fosters a culture of giving and support within the community, promoting a sense of unity and interconnectedness that transcends individual interests and concerns.

The practice of dana is a powerful expression of the values and principles of Buddhism, emphasizing the importance of compassion, generosity, and community. It provides a foundation for the relationship between the monastic and lay communities, creating a supportive and interconnected network that sustains and nurtures the spiritual growth of all its members. By engaging in the practice of dana, individuals contribute to the well-being and harmony of the community, embodying the principles of the Dharma in their daily lives.

CHALLENGES AND ADAPTATIONS

Monastic life presents various challenges that require adaptation and resilience, both for individual monks and nuns and for the Sangha as a whole. One of the primary challenges is maintaining the balance between tradition and modernity. As society evolves, monastic communities must find ways to uphold their ancient teachings and practices while remaining relevant and responsive to contemporary issues and needs. This requires flexibility, creativity, and a willingness to engage with new ideas and perspectives.

Monastics also face the challenge of maintaining discipline and focus amidst the distractions and demands of modern life. The increasing pace and complexity of contemporary society can create pressure and stress, making it difficult to sustain the simplicity and detachment that are central to the monastic path. Monks and nuns must cultivate mindfulness and self-awareness to navigate these challenges, drawing on their training and practice to remain grounded and centered in their spiritual pursuits.

Another challenge for monastic communities is the need to foster inclusivity and diversity within the Sangha. As Buddhism spreads to different cultures and regions, the Sangha must embrace a wide range of perspectives and experiences while maintaining its core principles and values. This requires open-mindedness and a commitment to dialogue and understanding, ensuring that the monastic community remains a welcoming and supportive environment for all who seek to follow the path of the Dharma.

The relationship between the monastic and lay communities also presents challenges, particularly regarding communication and understanding. As lay practitioners become more involved in the spiritual and social life of the community, monastics must find ways to engage and collaborate with them while maintaining their distinct roles and responsibilities. This requires clear communication, mutual respect, and a shared commitment to the values and principles of Buddhism.

In the face of these challenges, the Sangha must remain adaptable and resilient, drawing on its rich tradition of wisdom and practice to navigate the complexities of modern life. By embracing change and innovation while maintaining its core values and principles, the monastic community can continue to fulfill its role as a source of spiritual guidance and inspiration. Through this process of adaptation and growth, the Sangha remains a vital and dynamic force within the Buddhist community, capable of meeting the needs and aspirations of contemporary practitioners.

MEDITATION PRACTICES

IMPORTANCE OF MEDITATION IN THERAVADA

Meditation holds a central place in Theravada Buddhism. It's not just about sitting quietly; it's about transforming the mind. In Theravada, meditation is seen as the key to achieving enlightenment, the ultimate goal of Buddhist practice. The Buddha himself reached enlightenment through meditation, and his teachings emphasize its importance for anyone seeking spiritual growth.

For Theravada Buddhists, meditation serves as a tool for developing mindfulness and insight. It helps practitioners observe their thoughts and feelings without getting caught up in them. This process of observation leads to a deeper understanding of the nature of reality. Meditation helps individuals see things as they truly are, free from the distortions of desire and aversion.

Meditation also plays a crucial role in cultivating ethical conduct and mental discipline. Through meditation, practitioners learn to control their minds and develop positive qualities like compassion and patience. It helps them stay focused and calm, even in challenging situations. This mental discipline supports other aspects of the Buddhist path, such as following ethical precepts and engaging in wholesome actions.

The practice of meditation is deeply rooted in the daily lives of monks and nuns. It shapes their routines and guides their interactions with others. For laypeople, meditation provides a way to connect more deeply with the teachings and apply them in everyday life. Whether in a monastery or at home, meditation is a cornerstone of Theravada practice.

Meditation's importance in Theravada Buddhism can't be overstated. It's the means by which practitioners transform their minds and cultivate the qualities needed for enlightenment. Through regular meditation practice, they develop mindfulness, insight, and mental discipline, which are essential for following the Buddhist path.

SAMATHA (CALM) MEDITATION

Samatha meditation, or calm meditation, is a practice that focuses on developing deep concentration and tranquility. The goal is to quiet the mind and achieve a state of calmness and stability. Practitioners usually begin by concentrating on a single object, such as the breath, a mantra, or a visual object like a candle flame. This focus helps to settle the mind and reduce distractions.

One of the primary techniques in Samatha meditation is breath awareness. Practitioners pay close attention to the sensations of breathing, noticing the inhalation and exhalation without trying to change them. This simple yet powerful practice helps to anchor the mind and bring it into the present moment. Over time, the mind becomes more focused and less prone to wandering.

Another technique in Samatha meditation involves the use of a mantra or repeated phrase. This could be a word or phrase that has spiritual significance, such as "peace" or "loving-kindness." Repeating the mantra helps to occupy the mind and prevent distracting thoughts. It creates a rhythm that can lead to deeper states of concentration and tranquility.

Visualization is another method used in Samatha meditation. Practitioners might visualize a peaceful scene, such as a serene lake or a beautiful flower. This mental image serves as the focus of concentration, helping to calm the mind and evoke feelings of peace. Visualization can be particularly helpful for those who find it difficult to concentrate on more abstract objects like the breath.

The practice of Samatha meditation leads to the development of mental stability and clarity. As the mind becomes calmer, practitioners can experience states of deep peace and joy. These states of calm are not the ultimate goal but serve as a foundation for deeper insight practices. Samatha meditation helps to prepare the mind for the more advanced practice of Vipassana, or insight meditation.

LAUREN CHRISTENSEN

VIPASSANA (INSIGHT) MEDITATION

Vipassana meditation, also known as insight meditation, is a practice aimed at developing profound understanding and wisdom. Unlike Samatha meditation, which focuses on calming the mind, Vipassana involves observing the true nature of reality. The goal is to gain insight into the impermanent, unsatisfactory, and selfless nature of all phenomena. This understanding leads to liberation from suffering.

In Vipassana meditation, practitioners observe their thoughts, feelings, and sensations as they arise and pass away. The focus is on seeing things clearly and objectively, without attachment or aversion. By observing the changing nature of their experiences, practitioners come to understand the impermanence of all things. This insight helps to reduce attachment and craving, which are the root causes of suffering.

One of the key techniques in Vipassana meditation is body scanning. Practitioners systematically observe sensations throughout the body, from head to toe. They note each sensation without reacting to it, whether it's pleasant, unpleasant, or neutral. This practice helps to develop equanimity and detachment as practitioners learn to observe sensations without identifying with them.

Mindfulness of breathing is also central to Vipassana practice. Practitioners pay close attention to the breath, observing its natural rhythm and flow. They note the arising and passing away of each breath, which helps to cultivate awareness of the present moment. This mindfulness extends to other activities, such as walking, eating, and daily tasks, turning every moment into an opportunity for insight.

The practice of Vipassana leads to profound insights into the nature of existence. Practitioners come to see that all phenomena are impermanent, unsatisfactory, and without a permanent self. This understanding helps to dissolve the illusions that cause suffering. Through regular practice, Vipassana meditators develop greater wisdom, compassion, and inner peace, moving closer to the goal of enlightenment.

COMMON MEDITATION TECHNIQUES

Theravada Buddhism offers a variety of meditation techniques that practitioners can use to develop mindfulness, concentration, and insight. These techniques cater to different needs and preferences, allowing individuals to find a practice that resonates with them. While each technique has its unique focus, they all share the common goal of fostering spiritual growth and transformation.

One widely practiced technique is breath awareness, where practitioners focus on the sensations of breathing. This practice helps to anchor the mind and develop concentration. By observing the breath, practitioners cultivate mindfulness and learn to stay present in the moment. This technique is accessible to beginners and provides a strong foundation for more advanced practices.

Loving-kindness meditation, or Metta Bhavana, is another popular technique. In this practice, practitioners generate feelings of loving-kindness and compassion toward themselves and others. They repeat phrases like "May I be happy, may I be healthy, may I be safe," extending these wishes to friends, family, and even those they find challenging. This practice helps to cultivate a compassionate heart and reduce feelings of anger and resentment.

Body scanning is a technique often used in Vipassana meditation. Practitioners systematically observe sensations throughout the body, noting each one without attachment or aversion. This practice helps to develop equanimity and detachment as practitioners learn to observe sensations without reacting to them. Body scanning fosters a deep awareness of the body's processes and promotes a balanced mind.

Walking meditation is a practice that combines mindfulness with movement. Practitioners walk slowly and deliberately, paying close attention to the sensations of walking. They observe the lifting, moving, and placing of each foot, cultivating mindfulness with each step. This technique helps to integrate mindfulness into daily activities and provides a break from sitting meditation.

Visualization is another effective meditation technique. Practitioners create a mental image of a peaceful scene or an inspiring figure, such as the Buddha. This visualization serves as a focal point for concentration, helping to calm the mind and evoke positive feelings. Visualization can be particularly helpful for those who find it challenging to concentrate on abstract objects like the breath.

These common meditation techniques offer a range of approaches for developing mindfulness, concentration, and insight. By exploring different practices, individuals can find a technique that suits their needs and supports their spiritual journey. Whether through breath awareness, loving-kindness, body scanning, walking, or visualization, these techniques provide valuable tools for cultivating a mindful and compassionate life.

ROLE OF MEDITATION RETREATS

Meditation retreats play a crucial role in deepening one's practice and understanding of the Dharma. These retreats offer a dedicated time and space for intensive meditation, free from the distractions and responsibilities of daily life. Participants immerse themselves in a structured schedule of meditation, teachings, and silence, allowing for deep reflection and insight. Retreats provide an opportunity to deepen one's practice and experience the transformative power of meditation.

One of the primary benefits of meditation retreats is the opportunity for sustained, focused practice. In everyday life, it can be challenging to find the time and mental space for extended meditation sessions. Retreats offer a supportive environment where practitioners can dedicate themselves fully to their practice. This sustained effort allows for deeper concentration and mindfulness, leading to profound insights and personal growth.

Retreats also provide the guidance and support of experienced teachers. These teachers offer instructions, answer questions, and provide encouragement, helping participants navigate the challenges of intensive practice. The presence of a teacher can be especially valuable during difficult moments, offering reassurance and guidance. This support helps to create a safe and nurturing environment for exploration and growth.

Silence is a key component of many meditation retreats. By observing silence, participants minimize distractions and create a space for deep inner reflection. Silence allows for a heightened awareness of thoughts, feelings, and sensations, fostering a deeper understanding of the mind. This practice helps to cultivate mindfulness and insight, as practitioners observe the arising and passing away of mental and physical phenomena.

The sense of community on a meditation retreat can also be a powerful source of support. Practicing alongside others who share a common goal creates a sense of connection and solidarity. The collective energy of the group can enhance individual practice, providing motivation and inspiration. This sense of community fosters a supportive and encouraging environment, helping participants stay committed to their practice.

Meditation retreats offer a unique opportunity for intensive practice and deep reflection. By providing a dedicated time and space for meditation, retreats help practitioners deepen their understanding of the Dharma and experience the transformative power of mindfulness and insight. With the guidance of experienced teachers and the support of a like-minded community, participants can cultivate the qualities necessary for spiritual growth and liberation.

BENEFITS AND CHALLENGES

Meditation offers numerous benefits, but it also comes with its own set of challenges. Understanding both the rewards and difficulties of meditation can help practitioners develop a realistic and balanced approach to their practice. By acknowledging the benefits and challenges, individuals can cultivate perseverance and resilience, essential qualities for success on the spiritual path.

One of the primary benefits of meditation is the development of mindfulness and awareness. Through regular practice, individuals learn to observe their thoughts, feelings, and sensations without attachment or aversion. This increased awareness fosters a sense of clarity and insight, helping practitioners understand the nature of their minds. Mindfulness can improve focus, concentration, and emotional regulation, enhancing overall well-being and resilience.

Meditation also promotes emotional balance and stress reduction. By cultivating mindfulness, practitioners learn to respond to challenging situations with equanimity and composure. This ability to remain calm and centered in the face of adversity can lead to a greater sense of peace and contentment. Meditation has been shown to reduce stress, anxiety, and depression, offering a valuable tool for improving mental health.

Despite its benefits, meditation can be challenging, especially for beginners. Many people struggle with restlessness, boredom, or discomfort during meditation sessions. The mind may wander frequently, making it difficult to maintain focus and concentration. These challenges are natural and common, but they can be frustrating and discouraging for those new to meditation.

Another challenge of meditation is the surfacing of unresolved emotions or past experiences. As practitioners become more aware of their thoughts and feelings, they may encounter difficult or uncomfortable emotions. This process can be unsettling, but it is also an opportunity for healing and growth. By facing these emotions with mindfulness and compassion, practitioners can develop greater understanding and acceptance.

The practice of meditation requires patience, persistence, and dedication. Progress may be slow, and results may not be immediately apparent. It can be challenging to maintain a consistent practice amidst the demands of daily life. However, by cultivating discipline and commitment, practitioners can overcome these obstacles and experience the transformative power of meditation.

Meditation offers numerous benefits for mental, emotional, and spiritual well-being, but it also presents challenges that require perseverance and resilience. By understanding and embracing these challenges, individuals can develop a balanced and realistic approach to their practice. Through regular meditation, practitioners can cultivate mindfulness, insight, and emotional balance, leading to a more peaceful and fulfilling life.

INTEGRATION WITH DAILY LIFE

Integrating meditation into daily life is essential for cultivating mindfulness and awareness in every moment. While formal meditation practice is valuable, its true benefits are realized when applied to everyday activities. By bringing mindfulness to daily tasks and interactions, individuals can transform their lives and deepen their understanding of the Dharma. This integration fosters a continuous and dynamic practice that supports spiritual growth and transformation.

One way to integrate meditation into daily life is through the practice of mindfulness. Mindfulness involves paying attention to the present moment with an open and non-judgmental attitude. This practice can be applied to various activities, such as eating, walking, or working. By being fully present in each moment, individuals can develop greater awareness and appreciation of their experiences.

Another approach to integration is incorporating short meditation sessions throughout the day. Taking a few moments to pause and breathe can help to ground and center the mind. This practice can be particularly helpful during stressful or challenging situations, providing a sense of calm and clarity. By making meditation a regular part of the day, individuals can cultivate a more balanced and resilient mind.

Mindful communication is another important aspect of integrating meditation into daily life. By practicing mindful listening and speaking, individuals can improve their relationships and interactions with others. This involves being fully present and attentive during conversations, avoiding distractions, and responding with empathy and understanding. Mindful communication fosters connection and understanding, promoting harmony and compassion in relationships.

The integration of meditation into daily life also involves applying the insights and lessons learned in formal practice. Meditation helps to cultivate qualities such as patience, compassion, and gratitude, which can be applied to everyday situations. By embodying these qualities, individuals can navigate life's challenges with greater ease and equanimity. This integration supports a holistic approach to spiritual practice, where meditation is not separate from life but an integral part of it.

Integrating meditation into daily life is essential for realizing its full benefits and fostering spiritual growth. By cultivating mindfulness and awareness in everyday activities, individuals can transform their lives and deepen their understanding of the Dharma. This integration supports a continuous and dynamic practice that enriches all aspects of life, leading to a more peaceful, compassionate, and fulfilling existence.

RITUALS AND FESTIVALS

MAJOR THERAVADA FESTIVALS

In Theravada Buddhism, festivals are vibrant occasions that bring communities together to celebrate key events in the Buddha's life and the principles of the Dharma. These festivals are not just about tradition; they serve as moments of reflection and spiritual renewal. One of the most important festivals is Vesak, celebrated during the full moon of May. It commemorates the birth, enlightenment, and passing away of the Buddha. Temples are beautifully decorated with lights and flowers, and people gather for meditation, chanting, and offerings.

Vesak is a time for practicing generosity and kindness, key values in Buddhism. People often engage in acts of charity, like giving food to the poor or releasing animals from captivity as a symbolic gesture of liberation. This festival also emphasizes community, as families and friends come together to share meals and stories. The atmosphere is joyful and contemplative, reminding everyone of the Buddha's teachings on compassion and wisdom.

Another major festival is Asalha Puja, or Dhamma Day, which marks the Buddha's first sermon at Deer Park in Sarnath. This sermon introduced the Four Noble Truths and the Noble Eightfold Path, laying the foundation for Buddhist practice. On this day, monks give teachings, and laypeople offer food and robes to the monastic community. The festival highlights the importance of the Dharma and encourages reflection on how it applies to daily life.

Magha Puja is celebrated on the full moon day of the third lunar month, commemorating the spontaneous gathering of 1,250 enlightened disciples to hear the Buddha preach. This festival emphasizes the ideals of harmony and unity within the Buddhist community. People participate in candlelit processions, meditation, and chanting, reflecting on the principles of non-violence and loving-kindness. It's a time to deepen one's commitment to the Buddhist path and to the community.

The Kathina ceremony is another significant event, marking the end of the monastic retreat season known as Vassa. During this festival, laypeople express their gratitude to the monastic community by offering new robes and other necessities. It is a time of mutual appreciation and support between monks and laypeople, reinforcing the bonds that sustain the Buddhist community. The festival symbolizes renewal and generosity, echoing the spirit of the monastic retreat.

RITUALS FOR BIRTH, MARRIAGE, AND DEATH

In Theravada Buddhism, rituals for life events like birth, marriage, and death are meaningful practices that connect people to the teachings of the Buddha. These rituals serve as reminders of impermanence, compassion, and the interconnectedness of all beings. Each ceremony is an opportunity to reflect on the values of Buddhism and to seek guidance and blessings from the monastic community.

The birth of a child is a joyful occasion, celebrated with a ceremony called Naming Day or Pabbajja. Parents bring their newborns to the temple, where monks offer blessings and chant protective suttas to ensure the child's well-being and happiness. The ceremony includes making offerings to the Buddha and the Sangha, emphasizing gratitude and the importance of community support. This ritual helps families start their journey with mindfulness and a strong connection to the Dharma.

Marriage ceremonies in Theravada Buddhism focus on commitment, love, and mutual support. While marriage is not considered a religious sacrament, couples often seek blessings from monks to start their married life with wisdom and compassion. The ceremony typically involves offering food and donations to the temple, followed by chanting and advice from the monks. The couple exchanges vows and gifts, reinforcing the values of partnership and respect.

Funeral rituals in Theravada Buddhism are deeply significant, as they honor the deceased and provide comfort to the grieving family. The ceremony usually takes place at a temple, where monks chant suttas and deliver teachings on impermanence and rebirth. The body is often cremated, symbolizing the return to the elements. Family members and friends gather to offer food and donations, dedicating the merit to the deceased to support their journey in the cycle of rebirth.

These rituals help individuals and families navigate life's transitions with mindfulness and compassion. They provide an opportunity to reflect on the teachings of the Buddha and to strengthen one's connection to the community and the Dharma. By participating in these ceremonies, people can find comfort and guidance during times of change and uncertainty, reinforcing the values that sustain the Buddhist path.

DAILY AND WEEKLY DEVOTIONAL PRACTICES

In Theravada Buddhism, daily and weekly devotional practices play a vital role in nurturing faith and commitment to the path. These practices provide a rhythm to daily life, helping individuals cultivate mindfulness, gratitude, and compassion. They offer a way to connect with the teachings and to develop a personal relationship with the Buddha, the Dharma, and the Sangha.

One of the most common daily practices is morning and evening chanting. Buddhists recite verses that praise the Buddha, reflect on the Dharma, and seek protection from the Sangha. This practice helps to set a positive tone for the day and provides a moment of reflection and mindfulness in the evening. Chanting is often accompanied by meditation, allowing individuals to deepen their awareness and concentration.

Offering food to monks is another important daily practice known as dana. Laypeople prepare and offer food to the monastic community, expressing gratitude and support for their spiritual guidance. This act of generosity fosters a sense of interconnectedness and mutual respect between monks and laypeople. It also serves as a reminder of the value of selflessness and the importance of supporting the spiritual community.

Weekly observance days, or Uposatha days, are a time for intensified practice and reflection. Buddhists gather at temples to participate in chanting, meditation, and Dharma talks. Lay practitioners may choose to observe additional precepts, such as refraining from eating after noon or practicing celibacy for the day. These observance days provide an opportunity to deepen one's practice and to connect with the community and the teachings.

In addition to formal practices, many Buddhists incorporate mindfulness into their daily activities. This involves paying attention to the present moment with awareness and acceptance, whether walking, eating, or working. By cultivating mindfulness, individuals can bring the teachings into everyday life, developing greater insight and compassion.

Daily and weekly devotional practices help individuals maintain a consistent connection to the Dharma and the community. They provide opportunities for reflection, generosity, and mindfulness, supporting spiritual growth and well-being. Through these practices, Buddhists cultivate the qualities necessary for following the path and experiencing the transformative power of the teachings.

ROLE OF TEMPLES AND STUPAS

Temples and stupas hold a central place in Theravada Buddhism, serving as spiritual and cultural hubs for communities. These sacred spaces provide a setting for meditation, teaching, and rituals, fostering a sense of connection to the Buddha, the Dharma, and the Sangha. Temples and stupas are not only places of worship; they are centers of learning, reflection, and community life.

Temples are often the heart of Buddhist communities, offering a place for daily practice, special ceremonies, and festivals. They provide a tranquil environment for meditation and chanting, allowing individuals to deepen their connection to the teachings. Monks and nuns reside in temples, offering guidance, teachings, and support to lay practitioners. This relationship between monastics and laypeople strengthens the community and reinforces the values of generosity and compassion.

Stupas, or pagodas, are sacred structures that contain relics of the Buddha or other important Buddhist figures. They symbolize the enlightened mind and serve as focal points for devotion and reflection. Pilgrims and devotees circumambulate stupas, offering flowers, incense, and prayers. This practice helps cultivate mindfulness and gratitude, reminding individuals of the Buddha's teachings and the path to enlightenment.

The architecture and art of temples and stupas are rich in symbolism and meaning. Intricate carvings, statues, and paintings depict scenes from the Buddha's life and teachings, providing inspiration and guidance. These artistic expressions serve as visual reminders of the Dharma, inviting contemplation and reflection. The beauty and serenity of temples and stupas create a sacred atmosphere that supports spiritual practice.

Temples and stupas also play a role in preserving and transmitting cultural traditions. They host festivals, ceremonies, and educational programs that bring communities together and celebrate shared values and heritage. By fostering a sense of belonging and identity, these sacred spaces contribute to the resilience and vitality of Buddhist communities.

Temples and stupas are essential to the spiritual and cultural life of Theravada Buddhism. They provide a space for practice, reflection, and community, supporting individuals on their spiritual journey. Through their presence and activities, temples and stupas embody the teachings of the Buddha and inspire devotion, mindfulness, and compassion.

PILGRIMAGE SITES

Pilgrimage is an important aspect of Theravada Buddhism, offering an opportunity for reflection, renewal, and deepening one's connection to the teachings. Pilgrimage sites hold great significance as they are often associated with key events in the Buddha's life or contain relics of the Buddha and other enlightened beings. These sacred sites serve as focal points for devotion, meditation, and inspiration.

One of the most revered pilgrimage sites is Bodh Gaya in India, where the Buddha attained enlightenment under the Bodhi tree. Pilgrims from around the world visit this site to meditate, chant, and pay homage to the Buddha. The atmosphere at Bodh Gaya is one of profound reverence and tranquility, providing an ideal setting for deep reflection and spiritual growth. The site encourages visitors to cultivate mindfulness and insight, drawing on the energy and inspiration of the Buddha's enlightenment.

Another significant site is Sarnath, where the Buddha delivered his first sermon, setting the Wheel of Dharma in motion. Pilgrims gather at Sarnath to reflect on the Buddha's teachings and to participate in meditation and chanting. The site is a reminder of the importance of the Dharma and the transformative power of the teachings. It serves as an inspiration for practitioners to deepen their understanding and commitment to the path.

Kushinagar, where the Buddha passed into Parinirvana, is also a revered pilgrimage site. Pilgrims visit Kushinagar to pay their respects and to reflect on the impermanence and interconnectedness of all things. The site offers a space for contemplation and introspection, encouraging visitors to cultivate mindfulness and compassion. It serves as a reminder of the Buddha's teachings on liberation and the potential for awakening.

In addition to these major sites, there are numerous other pilgrimage locations throughout Asia, each with its unique history and significance. These sites offer opportunities for reflection, learning, and connection with the broader Buddhist community. Pilgrimage provides a chance to deepen one's practice and to draw inspiration from the sacred places and the community of fellow practitioners.

Pilgrimage is a powerful and transformative experience in Theravada Buddhism. It offers an opportunity for spiritual renewal, reflection, and connection with the teachings and the broader Buddhist community. By visiting sacred sites and engaging in practice, pilgrims can deepen their understanding of the Dharma and strengthen their commitment to the path of awakening.

CULTURAL VARIATIONS IN RITUALS

Theravada Buddhism has spread across various cultures and regions, leading to diverse interpretations and expressions of rituals. While the core teachings and principles remain consistent, the way rituals are practiced can vary significantly. These cultural variations reflect the unique histories, traditions, and values of different communities, enriching the tapestry of Theravada Buddhism and making it accessible to a wide range of people.

In Thailand, for example, Theravada rituals often incorporate vibrant festivals and ceremonies that reflect the country's rich cultural heritage. The Loy Krathong festival, celebrated on the full moon night of the twelfth lunar month, is a time for people to release small decorated floats on rivers, symbolizing the letting go of negativity and the cultivation of positive intentions. This festival combines Buddhist themes with traditional Thai customs, creating a unique and joyous celebration.

In Sri Lanka, Theravada rituals often emphasize devotion and generosity, reflecting the strong relationship between the monastic and lay communities. During Vesak, people create elaborate lanterns and decorations, transforming their homes and temples into vibrant displays of light. This celebration highlights the importance of community and the shared commitment to the teachings of the Buddha. Sri Lankan rituals often focus on the values of compassion and interconnectedness.

In Myanmar, Theravada rituals often involve the practice of meditation and the offering of food and other necessities to monks. The Thingyan Water Festival, marking the Burmese New Year, is a time for people to cleanse themselves of past misdeeds and start anew. This festival combines Buddhist themes of purification and renewal with traditional Burmese customs, creating a celebration that is both spiritual and cultural.

In Cambodia and Laos, Theravada rituals often emphasize the importance of family and community, reflecting the strong ties between the monastic and lay communities. The Pchum Ben festival, a time for honoring deceased ancestors, involves offering food and donations to monks, who in turn dedicate the merit to the departed. This festival highlights the interconnectedness of all beings and the importance of gratitude and generosity.

Cultural variations in Theravada rituals reflect the diverse ways in which communities engage with the teachings of the Buddha. These rituals provide opportunities for reflection, connection, and renewal, supporting individuals on their spiritual journey. By embracing these cultural expressions, Theravada Buddhism remains a dynamic and vibrant tradition, accessible to people from all walks of life and offering a path to spiritual growth and transformation.

CONTEMPORARY ADAPTATIONS

In the modern world, Theravada Buddhism continues to adapt and evolve, responding to the changing needs and contexts of contemporary practitioners. These adaptations reflect the tradition's resilience and ability to remain relevant, offering guidance and support for those seeking meaning and fulfillment in a rapidly changing world. Contemporary adaptations highlight the universality and timelessness of the Buddha's teachings, making them accessible and applicable to people from all walks of life.

One area of adaptation is the incorporation of technology into Buddhist practice. Many temples and monasteries now offer online meditation sessions, Dharma talks, and retreats, providing opportunities for people to engage with the teachings from the comfort of their own homes. These digital platforms allow individuals to connect with teachers and communities worldwide, fostering a sense of belonging and support. Technology has expanded access to the Dharma, making it more inclusive and accessible.

Another adaptation is the integration of Buddhist teachings with contemporary psychology and wellness practices. Mindfulness-based stress reduction (MBSR) and other mindfulness-based therapies draw on Buddhist principles to promote mental health and well-being. These programs have gained popularity in healthcare, education, and corporate settings, offering practical tools for managing stress and enhancing resilience. The integration of mindfulness into modern life reflects the adaptability and relevance of Buddhist teachings.

Contemporary practitioners also explore new ways of engaging with the Dharma, emphasizing social and environmental responsibility. Many Buddhists are actively involved in movements for social justice, environmental sustainability, and community service, applying the principles of compassion and interconnectedness to address global challenges. This emphasis on engaged Buddhism highlights the importance of taking the teachings beyond the meditation cushion and into the world, fostering positive change and transformation.

In addition to these adaptations, many contemporary practitioners seek to simplify and personalize their practice, focusing on the core principles of mindfulness, compassion, and wisdom. This approach allows individuals to tailor their practice to their unique needs and circumstances, making it more relevant and meaningful. By emphasizing the essence of the teachings, contemporary practitioners can cultivate a deeper connection to the Dharma and a greater sense of purpose and fulfillment.

Contemporary adaptations of Theravada Buddhism demonstrate the tradition's ability to remain dynamic and responsive to the changing world. By embracing new technologies, integrating with modern practices, and engaging with global challenges, Theravada Buddhism continues to offer guidance and inspiration for those seeking a path to wisdom and compassion. Through these adaptations, the teachings of the Buddha remain a vital and transformative force, accessible to people from all walks of life and offering a path to spiritual growth and liberation.

ETHICAL CONDUCT AND PRECEPTS

THE FIVE PRECEPTS FOR LAY BUDDHISTS

The Five Precepts are the foundation of ethical conduct in Theravada Buddhism, providing guidelines for laypeople to live by. These precepts are not strict commandments but voluntary commitments that individuals make to cultivate moral discipline and compassion. They serve as a framework for ethical living, helping people navigate the complexities of life with mindfulness and integrity. The Five Precepts offer a way to foster personal growth and contribute positively to society.

The first precept is to abstain from taking life. This commitment emphasizes the value of compassion and respect for all living beings. By refraining from harming others, individuals cultivate kindness and empathy, fostering a sense of interconnectedness with the world around them. This precept encourages people to consider the impact of their actions on others and to promote non-violence in their interactions.

The second precept is to abstain from taking what is not given. This principle promotes honesty and respect for others' property. By avoiding theft and dishonesty, individuals develop integrity and trustworthiness. This precept encourages people to value fairness and to respect the rights of others. It also highlights the importance of generosity and sharing, fostering a sense of community and cooperation.

The third precept is to abstain from sexual misconduct. This commitment emphasizes the importance of respect and responsibility in relationships. By refraining from actions that cause harm or suffering to others, individuals cultivate integrity and respect for the dignity of others. This precept encourages people to engage in healthy and respectful relationships, promoting trust and harmony in their interactions.

The fourth precept is to abstain from false speech. This principle emphasizes the value of truthfulness and honesty. By avoiding lies, gossip, and harmful speech, individuals cultivate honesty and integrity in their communication. This precept encourages people to speak with kindness and respect, promoting understanding and trust in their relationships. It also highlights the importance of mindful communication and the power of words to create positive change.

The fifth precept is to abstain from intoxicants that cloud the mind. This commitment emphasizes the importance of mindfulness and clarity in one's actions. By avoiding substances that impair judgment and awareness, individuals cultivate self-control and responsibility. This precept encourages people to live with mindfulness and awareness, promoting well-being and balance in their lives. It also highlights the importance of making conscious choices that support personal and collective well-being.

THE EIGHT PRECEPTS

The Eight Precepts are an extension of the Five Precepts, offering additional guidelines for lay practitioners who wish to deepen their practice and commitment to the Dharma. These precepts are often observed on special occasions, such as Uposatha days or during meditation retreats. They provide an opportunity for individuals to cultivate greater mindfulness, discipline, and detachment from worldly desires.

The first five precepts of the Eight Precepts are the same as the Five Precepts: abstaining from taking life, taking what is not given, sexual misconduct, false speech, and intoxicants. These foundational principles emphasize the importance of ethical conduct and mindfulness in daily life. By observing these precepts, individuals cultivate compassion, integrity, and responsibility, fostering personal growth and positive relationships.

The sixth precept is to abstain from eating at inappropriate times. This commitment encourages individuals to cultivate self-discipline and moderation in their consumption. By refraining from eating after midday, practitioners develop mindfulness and awareness of their bodily needs. This precept promotes simplicity and detachment from sensory pleasures, fostering a sense of inner peace and balance.

The seventh precept is to abstain from entertainment and beautification. This principle emphasizes the importance of detachment from worldly distractions and desires. By avoiding entertainment and adornment, individuals cultivate mindfulness and focus on their spiritual practice. This precept encourages people to prioritize inner development over external appearances, fostering a sense of contentment and simplicity.

The eighth precept is to abstain from using luxurious beds and seats. This commitment encourages individuals to cultivate humility and simplicity in their living conditions. By avoiding comfort and luxury, practitioners develop mindfulness and appreciation for the present moment. This precept promotes detachment from material possessions and fosters a sense of gratitude and contentment.

The Eight Precepts provide an opportunity for individuals to deepen their practice and commitment to the Dharma. By observing these guidelines, practitioners cultivate mindfulness, discipline, and detachment from worldly desires, supporting their spiritual growth and development. The Eight Precepts offer a framework for ethical living that fosters personal well-being and contributes to a harmonious and compassionate society.

THE TEN PRECEPTS FOR NOVICES

The Ten Precepts for novices in Theravada Buddhism are a set of ethical guidelines that provide a foundation for monastic training and practice. These precepts offer a framework for developing mindfulness, discipline, and detachment from worldly desires. For novices, observing the Ten Precepts is a commitment to cultivating ethical conduct and spiritual growth.

The first five precepts for novices are the same as the Five Precepts for laypeople: abstaining from taking life, taking what is not given, sexual misconduct, false speech, and intoxicants. These foundational principles emphasize the importance of ethical conduct and mindfulness in daily life. By observing these precepts, novices cultivate compassion, integrity, and responsibility, fostering personal growth and positive relationships.

The sixth precept is to abstain from eating at inappropriate times, usually after midday. This commitment encourages novices to cultivate self-discipline and moderation in their consumption. By refraining from eating after midday, practitioners develop mindfulness and awareness of their bodily needs. This precept promotes simplicity and detachment from sensory pleasures, fostering a sense of inner peace and balance.

The seventh precept is to abstain from dancing, singing, music, and entertainment. This principle emphasizes the importance of detachment from worldly distractions and desires. By avoiding entertainment and adornment, novices cultivate mindfulness and focus on their spiritual practice. This precept encourages individuals to prioritize inner development over external appearances, fostering a sense of contentment and simplicity.

The eighth precept is to abstain from wearing garlands, perfumes, and personal adornments. This commitment encourages novices to cultivate humility and simplicity in their appearance. By avoiding adornments and perfumes, practitioners develop mindfulness and appreciation for the present moment. This precept promotes detachment from material possessions and fosters a sense of gratitude and contentment.

The ninth precept is to abstain from using luxurious and high seats and beds. This principle encourages novices to cultivate humility and simplicity in their living conditions. By avoiding comfort and luxury, practitioners develop mindfulness and appreciation for the present moment. This precept promotes detachment from material possessions and fosters a sense of gratitude and contentment.

The tenth precept is to abstain from accepting gold and silver, or money. This commitment encourages novices to cultivate detachment from material wealth and possessions. By avoiding the use of money, practitioners develop a sense of reliance on the generosity of the lay community and foster a spirit of gratitude and humility. This precept promotes detachment from material desires and supports the development of a contented and simple lifestyle.

The Ten Precepts for novices provide a foundation for monastic training and practice, offering guidelines for developing mindfulness, discipline, and detachment from worldly desires. By observing these precepts, novices cultivate ethical conduct and spiritual growth, supporting their journey on the path to awakening.

THE ROLE OF SILA (MORALITY) IN PRACTICE

In Theravada Buddhism, sila, or morality, plays a central role in the practice and development of the spiritual path. Sila refers to ethical conduct and moral discipline, providing a foundation for cultivating mindfulness, concentration, and wisdom. By observing the precepts and cultivating virtuous qualities, individuals create the conditions for personal growth and spiritual development.

Sila is the first of the threefold training in Buddhism, which consists of sila (morality), samadhi (concentration), and panna (wisdom). This sequence reflects the importance of ethical conduct as the foundation for the development of concentration and wisdom. By cultivating sila, individuals purify their actions, speech, and thoughts, creating a conducive environment for meditation and insight.

The practice of sila involves observing the precepts and cultivating virtuous qualities such as compassion, honesty, and generosity. By adhering to these principles, individuals develop a sense of responsibility and integrity in their actions. This ethical conduct fosters positive relationships and contributes to a harmonious and compassionate society.

Sila also plays a crucial role in the development of mindfulness and concentration. By cultivating ethical conduct, individuals reduce distractions and disturbances in their minds, allowing for greater focus and clarity. This mental clarity supports the practice of meditation, enabling practitioners to develop deeper concentration and insight.

The practice of sila is not limited to observing the precepts but involves the cultivation of positive mental states and the development of wholesome habits. By fostering qualities such as loving-kindness, patience, and gratitude, individuals create the conditions for spiritual growth and transformation. This cultivation of virtuous qualities supports the development of wisdom and insight, leading to the realization of the ultimate goal of enlightenment.

The role of sila in practice is essential for the development of the spiritual path. By cultivating ethical conduct and virtuous qualities, individuals create the conditions for personal growth and spiritual development. The practice of sila supports the development of mindfulness, concentration, and wisdom, fostering a harmonious and compassionate society.

ETHICAL CHALLENGES IN MODERN TIMES

In the modern world, ethical challenges present complex and multifaceted issues for individuals seeking to uphold the principles of sila. The rapid pace of technological advancement, globalization, and social change has created new ethical dilemmas and uncertainties. These challenges require a flexible and adaptive approach to ethical conduct, drawing on the timeless principles of the Dharma to navigate the complexities of contemporary life.

One of the significant ethical challenges in modern times is the impact of technology on communication and relationships. The rise of social media and digital communication has transformed how people interact and connect, often blurring the lines between public and private life. This shift raises questions about the ethical use of technology, the importance of mindful communication, and the impact of digital interactions on relationships and well-being.

Another ethical challenge is the increasing awareness of social and environmental issues, such as climate change, inequality, and injustice. These global challenges require individuals to consider the ethical implications of their actions and choices, from consumption habits to social and political engagement. The principles of sila provide a framework for addressing these issues, emphasizing the importance of compassion, responsibility, and interconnectedness.

The modern workplace also presents ethical challenges as individuals navigate issues such as corporate responsibility, transparency, and work-life balance. The principles of sila encourage individuals to cultivate honesty, integrity, and fairness in their professional lives, fostering positive relationships and contributing to a supportive and ethical work environment.

In addition to these challenges, individuals face ethical dilemmas in their personal lives, such as balancing personal desires with responsibilities to family and community. The principles of sila offer guidance for navigating these complexities, encouraging individuals to cultivate mindfulness, compassion, and integrity in their actions and decisions.

Ethical challenges in modern times require individuals to draw on the principles of sila and the teachings of the Dharma to navigate the complexities of contemporary life. By cultivating mindfulness, compassion, and integrity, individuals can address these challenges with wisdom and resilience, contributing to a harmonious and compassionate society.

THE IMPACT OF ETHICAL CONDUCT ON SOCIETY

The impact of ethical conduct on society is profound and far-reaching, influencing the well-being and harmony of communities and individuals. In Theravada Buddhism, the practice of sila, or morality, is seen as a cornerstone for creating a compassionate and just society. By cultivating ethical conduct and virtuous qualities, individuals contribute to the development of a harmonious and interconnected world.

Ethical conduct promotes trust and cooperation within communities, fostering positive relationships and social cohesion. By adhering to the principles of honesty, compassion, and respect, individuals create an environment of mutual support and understanding. This foundation of trust and cooperation strengthens communities, promoting resilience and adaptability in the face of challenges.

The practice of ethical conduct also supports the development of social and environmental responsibility. By cultivating awareness of the interconnectedness of all beings, individuals are encouraged to consider the impact of their actions on others and the environment. This awareness fosters a sense of responsibility and stewardship, promoting sustainable and equitable practices that benefit both present and future generations.

Ethical conduct also plays a crucial role in addressing social and economic inequalities and promoting fairness and justice in society. By emphasizing the importance of compassion, generosity, and empathy, individuals are encouraged to engage in acts of service and support for those in need. This commitment to social justice and equality fosters a sense of solidarity and interconnectedness, contributing to the well-being of all members of society.

The impact of ethical conduct on society extends to the development of a culture of mindfulness and reflection. By encouraging individuals to cultivate mindfulness and awareness, the principles of sila promote self-reflection and personal growth. This culture of mindfulness fosters a deeper understanding of the self and others, promoting empathy, compassion, and understanding in interactions and relationships.

The impact of ethical conduct on society is transformative and far-reaching, fostering trust, cooperation, and responsibility within communities. By cultivating the principles of sila and the teachings of the Dharma, individuals contribute to the development of a harmonious and compassionate society, promoting well-being and justice for all members of the community.

THERAVADA IN DIFFERENT CULTURES

THERAVADA IN SRI LANKA

Sri Lanka is often considered the cradle of Theravada Buddhism, where the tradition has been preserved and practiced for over two millennia. The story of Theravada Buddhism in Sri Lanka began in the 3rd century BCE when the Indian Emperor Ashoka sent his son Mahinda to the island to spread the teachings of the Buddha. The king of Sri Lanka at the time, Devanampiya Tissa, embraced the teachings, and Buddhism quickly became the dominant religion on the island.

The influence of Theravada Buddhism in Sri Lanka extends beyond religious practice and deeply into the country's culture, politics, and social fabric. Monasteries and temples have been centers of learning, preserving not only the religious texts but also the Sinhalese language and literature. This integration of Buddhism into the cultural identity of Sri

Lanka has helped maintain the tradition's continuity and relevance over the centuries.

The Sangha, or monastic community, plays a crucial role in Sri Lankan society. Monks are highly respected figures, often consulted for guidance on moral and social issues. The relationship between the laity and the monastic community is one of mutual support; laypeople provide material support to the monks, who, in turn, offer spiritual guidance and teachings. This interdependence strengthens the community and reinforces the values of generosity and compassion.

Theravada Buddhism in Sri Lanka is also characterized by vibrant festivals and rituals that mark important events in the Buddhist calendar. Vesak, celebrating the birth, enlightenment, and death of the Buddha, is a major event where streets are adorned with lanterns and devotees engage in acts of generosity and devotion. These festivals are not only religious observances but also cultural celebrations that bring communities together in a shared expression of faith and tradition.

Despite challenges such as colonialism and modernization, Theravada Buddhism in Sri Lanka remains a vital and dynamic tradition. The resilience of the practice can be attributed to its deep roots in the culture and its adaptability to changing times. By preserving the core teachings while embracing new influences, Sri Lankan Theravada Buddhism continues to thrive, offering a path of peace and wisdom to its followers.

LAUREN CHRISTENSEN

THERAVADA IN THAILAND

In Thailand, Theravada Buddhism is not just a religion; it is a way of life. Approximately 95% of the Thai population identifies as Buddhist, and the influence of the religion is evident in every aspect of society, from government and education to art and architecture. The history of Theravada Buddhism in Thailand dates back to the 13th century, during the Sukhothai Kingdom, when it became the state religion.

One of the most striking features of Thai Buddhism is its integration with Thai culture and traditions. The Sangha, or monastic community, holds a significant place in Thai society, with monks often serving as community leaders and advisors. Monasteries function as centers of education and social support, providing schooling for children and guidance for adults. This integration of monastic life with community life strengthens social bonds and reinforces the values of compassion and mindfulness.

Thai Buddhism is also known for its elaborate rituals and ceremonies, which often blend Buddhist teachings with local customs. For example, the annual Kathina ceremony, where laypeople offer robes and other necessities to monks, is a vibrant and communal event. These ceremonies are opportunities for the community to come together, express devotion, and reinforce their commitment to the Dharma. They highlight the importance of generosity and the interconnectedness of all beings.

Meditation is a central practice in Thai Buddhism, with many monasteries offering retreats and courses for both monks and laypeople. The focus is often on Vipassana, or insight meditation, which aims to cultivate mindfulness and awareness of the present moment. This emphasis on meditation reflects the Thai Buddhist belief in the importance of direct experience and personal insight in achieving enlightenment.

The resilience and adaptability of Thai Buddhism are evident in its response to modern challenges. While maintaining its core teachings, Thai Buddhism has embraced new technologies and approaches to education, ensuring its relevance in contemporary society. This adaptability, coupled with its deep cultural roots, ensures that Theravada Buddhism in Thailand remains a vibrant and influential tradition, offering guidance and inspiration to its followers.

THERAVADA IN MYANMAR (BURMA)

Theravada Buddhism is deeply woven into the fabric of Myanmar's cultural and social identity. Known as the "Land of Pagodas," Myanmar is home to thousands of Buddhist temples and stupas, reflecting the profound influence of Buddhism on the country's landscape and way of life. The tradition was established in Myanmar over a thousand years ago and has since become a defining element of the nation's identity.

The monastic community in Myanmar plays a central role in society, with monks and nuns regarded as spiritual leaders and educators. The tradition of offering alms to monks is a daily practice for many Burmese people, symbolizing the interdependence between the monastic and lay communities. This relationship is built on mutual respect and generosity, with laypeople supporting the monastics who, in turn, provide spiritual guidance and teachings.

In Myanmar, meditation is a highly valued practice, with many monasteries and meditation centers offering retreats and courses to both monks and laypeople. The focus is often on Vipassana, or insight meditation, which aims to cultivate mindfulness and insight into the nature of reality. This emphasis on meditation reflects the Burmese belief in the transformative power of personal experience and direct realization of the Dharma.

Buddhist festivals and rituals are an integral part of life in Myanmar, with celebrations such as Thingyan, the Burmese New Year, drawing on Buddhist themes of renewal and purification. These festivals are opportunities for communities to come together in a spirit of joy and reflection, reinforcing the values of compassion, generosity, and mindfulness. They highlight the interconnectedness of all beings and the importance of living in harmony with others.

Despite challenges such as political unrest and economic difficulties, Theravada Buddhism in Myanmar remains a resilient and dynamic tradition. Its deep cultural roots and adaptability ensure its continued relevance in contemporary society. By preserving the core teachings of the Buddha while embracing new influences, Burmese Buddhism offers a path of peace and wisdom for its followers.

THERAVADA IN CAMBODIA AND LAOS

In Cambodia and Laos, Theravada Buddhism is a vital and enduring tradition that shapes the cultural and social identity of both countries. The roots of Theravada Buddhism in these regions can be traced back to the 13th century when it was established as the dominant religious tradition. Since then, Buddhism has been a cornerstone of the cultural, spiritual, and political life of these countries.

The monastic community, or Sangha, plays a crucial role in both Cambodia and Laos, serving as spiritual leaders, educators, and community advisors. Monasteries are often the center of village life, providing education, healthcare, and social support. This integration of monastic life with community life fosters a strong sense of interconnectedness and mutual support, reinforcing the values of generosity and compassion.

In Cambodia and Laos, Buddhist festivals and rituals are significant cultural events, reflecting the integration of Buddhist teachings with local traditions. The Cambodian New Year, or Chaul Chnam Thmey, is a vibrant celebration that combines Buddhist ceremonies with traditional customs, such as water-splashing and games. Similarly, the Lao New Year, or Pi Mai, is marked by processions, offerings, and temple visits. These festivals highlight the importance of community and cultural identity in the practice of Buddhism.

Meditation is a valued practice in both countries, with many monasteries offering retreats and courses for both monks and laypeople. The focus is often on Vipassana, or insight meditation, which aims to cultivate mindfulness and awareness of the present moment. This emphasis on meditation reflects the belief in the transformative power of personal experience and direct realization of the Dharma.

Despite challenges such as economic difficulties and the legacy of conflict, Theravada Buddhism in Cambodia and Laos remains a vibrant and dynamic tradition. Its deep cultural roots and adaptability ensure its continued relevance in contemporary society. By preserving the core teachings of the Buddha while embracing new influences, Buddhism in these regions offers a path of peace and wisdom for its followers.

THERAVADA IN OTHER PARTS OF THE WORLD

Theravada Buddhism has extended beyond its traditional roots in Southeast Asia to become a global tradition, with communities and practitioners across Europe, North America, and other regions. This spread has been facilitated by increased travel, communication, and the efforts of dedicated teachers and practitioners who have introduced the teachings to new audiences. As a result, Theravada Buddhism has adapted to new cultural contexts, offering guidance and inspiration to people from diverse backgrounds.

In the West, Theravada Buddhism has gained popularity, particularly for its emphasis on meditation and mindfulness practices. Many Westerners have been drawn to Vipassana, or insight meditation, which is valued for its practical benefits in stress reduction, emotional regulation, and personal growth. Meditation centers and retreats have sprung up across Europe and North America, providing opportunities for individuals to explore the teachings and deepen their practice.

Theravada communities in the West often reflect a blend of traditional practices and contemporary approaches. Temples and meditation centers serve as hubs for cultural exchange and community building, offering teachings, meditation sessions, and cultural events. These communities provide a space for individuals to connect with the teachings and with others who share a commitment to the path of awakening.

The adaptation of Theravada Buddhism in Western contexts has also led to new interpretations and expressions of the teachings. Western practitioners often explore the intersection of Buddhism with psychology, science, and social justice, drawing on the principles of the Dharma to address contemporary challenges. This exploration has led to innovative approaches to practice and a broader understanding of the teachings.

The global spread of Theravada Buddhism highlights its universality and adaptability, offering guidance and inspiration to people from diverse backgrounds and cultures. By embracing new influences and responding to the needs of contemporary practitioners, Theravada Buddhism continues to thrive as a dynamic and transformative tradition, offering a path of peace and wisdom to individuals worldwide.

CULTURAL INFLUENCES AND ADAPTATIONS

As Theravada Buddhism has spread to different cultures and regions, it has undergone various adaptations, reflecting the unique histories, traditions, and values of each community. These cultural influences have enriched the tradition, leading to diverse interpretations and expressions of the teachings. By embracing cultural diversity, Theravada Buddhism has remained a dynamic and relevant tradition, accessible to people from all walks of life.

In Sri Lanka, the integration of Buddhism with local customs and traditions has led to unique expressions of the teachings. The practice of offering food to monks, known as dana, is deeply ingrained in Sri Lankan culture, reflecting the values of generosity and interconnectedness. This tradition fosters a sense of community and mutual support, reinforcing the importance of ethical conduct and compassion in daily life.

In Thailand, the influence of Theravada Buddhism is evident in the country's art, architecture, and cultural practices. The elaborate rituals and ceremonies that mark important events in the Buddhist calendar often blend Buddhist teachings with local customs. This integration of Buddhism with Thai culture creates a unique and vibrant expression of the tradition, reflecting the values of harmony and interconnectedness.

In Myanmar, the emphasis on meditation and mindfulness practices reflects the influence of local traditions and beliefs. The practice of Vipassana, or insight meditation, is highly valued, with many monasteries offering retreats and courses for both monks and laypeople. This emphasis on meditation reflects the belief in the transformative power of personal experience and direct realization of the Dharma.

In the West, the adaptation of Theravada Buddhism has led to new interpretations and expressions of the teachings. Western practitioners often explore the intersection of Buddhism with psychology, science, and social justice, drawing on the principles of the Dharma to address contemporary challenges. This exploration has led to innovative approaches to practice and a broader understanding of the teachings.

The cultural influences and adaptations of Theravada Buddhism highlight its universality and adaptability, offering guidance and inspiration to people from diverse backgrounds and cultures. By embracing cultural diversity and responding to the needs of contemporary practitioners, Theravada Buddhism continues to thrive as a dynamic and transformative tradition, offering a path of peace and wisdom to individuals worldwide.

COMPARATIVE STUDY WITH OTHER BUDDHIST TRADITIONS

Theravada Buddhism is one of the three major traditions in Buddhism, alongside Mahayana and Vajrayana. While all three traditions share a common foundation in the teachings of the Buddha, they have distinct practices, beliefs, and interpretations of the Dharma. A comparative study of these traditions offers valuable insights into the diversity and richness of Buddhist thought and practice.

One of the primary differences between Theravada and Mahayana Buddhism is the emphasis on individual versus collective liberation. Theravada, often referred to as the "path of the elders," focuses on the individual's journey to enlightenment through personal practice and adherence to the monastic code. In contrast, Mahayana, known as the "greater vehicle," emphasizes the collective liberation of all beings and the ideal of the bodhisattva, who vows to attain enlightenment for the benefit of others.

Vajrayana Buddhism, also known as the "diamond vehicle," is an esoteric tradition that incorporates tantric practices and rituals. It emphasizes the use of visualization, mantra recitation, and deity yoga to achieve enlightenment. While Theravada focuses on the development of mindfulness and insight through meditation, Vajrayana practitioners engage in complex rituals and practices designed to transform the mind and body.

Despite these differences, all three traditions share a common foundation in the teachings of the Buddha, including the Four Noble Truths and the Eightfold Path. Each tradition offers unique methods and practices for cultivating mindfulness, wisdom, and compassion, reflecting the diverse ways in which individuals can engage with the Dharma.

The diversity of Buddhist traditions highlights the universality and adaptability of the teachings, offering guidance and inspiration to people from diverse backgrounds and cultures. By exploring the similarities and differences between these traditions, individuals can gain a deeper understanding of the Dharma and its potential for personal and social transformation. This comparative study offers a broader perspective on the richness and diversity of Buddhist thought and practice, fostering mutual respect and understanding among practitioners.

WOMEN IN THERAVADA BUDDHISM

HISTORICAL ROLE OF WOMEN

In the early days of Buddhism, women played a vital role in the spiritual community. The Buddha's decision to include women in his Sangha, or monastic community, was a groundbreaking move for his time. He established the Bhikkhuni Sangha, the order of nuns, allowing women to pursue the monastic path and attain enlightenment. This decision opened the door for women to participate in spiritual life and offered them the opportunity to contribute to the Buddhist community.

The inclusion of women in the monastic community was met with resistance from some of the Buddha's followers. Traditional views held that women were not suited for the monastic life, and there were concerns about the impact on the Sangha's purity and discipline. Despite this opposition, the Buddha maintained that women were capable of achieving the same spiritual goals as men. He established a set of rules, known as the Eight Garudhammas, to guide the relationship between monks and nuns and to ensure the harmony of the Sangha.

Historically, women in the Theravada tradition have made significant contributions as practitioners, teachers, and scholars. Many notable female disciples, such as Khema and Uppalavanna, were highly respected for their wisdom and insight. Their teachings and writings have been preserved in the Buddhist texts, inspiring generations of practitioners. These women demonstrated that the path to enlightenment is accessible to all, regardless of gender.

Despite the opportunities for spiritual practice, women in the Theravada tradition have faced challenges and limitations. Social and cultural norms often restricted their access to education and resources, making it difficult for them to fully participate in monastic life. The ordination of women as bhikkhunis, or fully ordained nuns, was discontinued in many Theravada countries for centuries, limiting their opportunities for spiritual growth and leadership.

Throughout history, women have played a crucial role in preserving and transmitting the teachings of the Buddha. Their dedication and resilience have ensured the continuity of the Theravada tradition, even in the face of adversity. By challenging societal norms and advocating for their right to practice, women have helped shape the spiritual landscape of Theravada Buddhism.

ORDINATION OF WOMEN

The ordination of women in Theravada Buddhism has been a complex and evolving issue. Initially, the Buddha's decision to ordain women was a radical step toward gender equality in spiritual practice. He established the Bhikkhuni Sangha, allowing women to pursue the monastic path alongside men. However, over time, the ordination of women faced challenges and opposition, leading to the decline and eventual disappearance of the Bhikkhuni Sangha in many Theravada countries.

The decline of the Bhikkhuni Sangha was influenced by cultural, social, and political factors. In many societies, traditional gender roles and expectations limited women's opportunities for education and spiritual practice. The loss of the bhikkhuni ordination lineage meant that women could only be ordained as novices, with limited access to the full monastic path. This restriction prevented women from fully participating in the spiritual community and limited their opportunities for leadership and influence.

In recent years, there has been a renewed interest in restoring the bhikkhuni ordination lineage. Efforts to revive the Bhikkhuni Sangha have been met with both support and resistance within the Theravada community. Some argue that the revival of the bhikkhuni ordination is essential for gender equality and the full inclusion of women in the spiritual community. Others express concerns about the validity of the ordination and its impact on the traditional monastic structure.

Several successful bhikkhuni ordinations have taken place in countries such as Sri Lanka and Thailand, where supportive monks and nuns have worked together to restore the lineage. These ordinations have sparked a broader conversation about the role of women in Buddhism and the importance of gender equality in spiritual practice. The revival of the

Bhikkhuni Sangha is seen as a significant step toward empowering women and promoting inclusivity within the Theravada tradition.

The ordination of women in Theravada Buddhism continues to be a topic of discussion and debate. While challenges remain, the efforts to restore the Bhikkhuni Sangha reflect a growing recognition of the importance of gender equality in spiritual practice. By advocating for their right to ordination, women are paving the way for a more inclusive and diverse Theravada community.

NOTABLE FEMALE PRACTITIONERS AND TEACHERS

Throughout the history of Theravada Buddhism, numerous women have made significant contributions as practitioners, teachers, and scholars. These women have demonstrated the potential for spiritual attainment and leadership, inspiring others with their dedication and wisdom. Their stories and teachings have become an integral part of the Theravada tradition, offering guidance and inspiration to generations of practitioners.

One of the earliest and most notable female practitioners in Theravada Buddhism is Mahapajapati Gotami, the Buddha's aunt and foster mother. She was the first woman to request ordination and became the leader of the Bhikkhuni Sangha. Her determination and leadership paved the way for countless women to pursue the monastic path, and her story continues to inspire women seeking spiritual fulfillment.

Another prominent figure is Khema, a disciple of the Buddha known for her wisdom and eloquence. Khema was a former queen who renounced her royal life to join the monastic community. She became one of the Buddha's chief female disciples and was renowned for her deep understanding of the Dharma. Her teachings and insights have been preserved in the Pali Canon, where they continue to inspire practitioners.

Dhammadinna is another notable female practitioner and teacher. She was highly esteemed for her understanding of the Dharma and her ability to teach and explain complex concepts with clarity. Her dialogues with lay practitioners are recorded in the Pali Canon, where she addresses questions about the path to enlightenment and the nature of the mind. Her teachings remain a valuable resource for those seeking to deepen their understanding of the Buddha's teachings.

In modern times, women such as Ayya Khema and Dipa Ma have gained recognition for their contributions to Theravada Buddhism. Ayya Khema was a German nun who played a significant role in reviving the Bhikkhuni Sangha and teaching meditation to Western audiences. Dipa Ma, a laywoman from India, was known for her profound meditation practice and her ability to teach mindfulness and insight to students around the world. Both women have inspired countless practitioners with their dedication and insight.

The contributions of these notable female practitioners and teachers highlight the potential for women to attain spiritual realization and offer valuable insights into the Dharma. Their stories and teachings serve as a source of inspiration and encouragement for women and men alike, demonstrating the transformative power of the Buddhist path.

CHALLENGES FACED BY WOMEN IN THE SANGHA

Women in the Theravada Sangha have faced numerous challenges, both historical and contemporary, as they strive to pursue the monastic path and contribute to the spiritual community. These challenges are rooted in cultural, social, and institutional factors that have limited women's opportunities for education, leadership, and ordination. Despite these obstacles, women have shown resilience and determination in their pursuit of spiritual growth and equality.

One of the primary challenges for women in the Sangha is the lack of access to full ordination. In many Theravada countries, the Bhikkhuni Sangha, or the order of fully ordained nuns, was lost centuries ago. This loss has limited women's opportunities for spiritual development and leadership within the monastic community. Without full ordination, women often face restrictions in their practice and are unable to participate fully in the monastic hierarchy.

Social and cultural norms also pose significant challenges for women in the Sangha. Traditional gender roles and expectations often limit women's opportunities for education and spiritual practice, making it difficult for them to pursue the monastic path. In some communities, women may face resistance or discrimination from family members or society, discouraging them from joining the monastic community or pursuing leadership roles.

Institutional barriers within the monastic community can also impede women's progress. The lack of resources and support for women's monastic education and training can limit their opportunities for growth and development. Additionally, the hierarchical structure of the Sangha can create power dynamics that disadvantage women, making it challenging for them to access leadership positions or participate in decision-making processes.

Despite these challenges, women in the Theravada Sangha have shown remarkable resilience and determination. Many have sought to overcome these obstacles by advocating for their rights, seeking education and training, and building supportive communities. Their efforts have contributed to the growing recognition of the importance of gender equality and the potential for women to contribute meaningfully to the Theravada tradition.

The challenges faced by women in the Sangha highlight the need for continued advocacy and support for gender equality within the Theravada community. By addressing these obstacles and creating opportunities for women to pursue the monastic path, the tradition can become more inclusive and diverse, benefiting the entire Buddhist community.

MODERN MOVEMENTS FOR GENDER EQUALITY

In recent years, there has been a growing movement for gender equality within Theravada Buddhism, driven by the recognition of the important role women play in the spiritual community. This movement seeks to address the historical and institutional barriers that have limited women's opportunities for ordination, education, and leadership. By advocating for gender equality, these modern movements aim to create a more inclusive and diverse Theravada tradition.

One of the key focuses of the movement for gender equality is the revival of the Bhikkhuni Sangha. Efforts to restore the ordination of women have gained momentum in countries such as Sri Lanka, Thailand, and Myanmar, where supportive monks and nuns have worked together to reinstate the lineage. These ordinations have been met with both support and resistance within the Theravada community, sparking important conversations about the role of women in Buddhism.

Organizations and individuals have played a significant role in advocating for gender equality within the Theravada tradition. Groups such as Sakyadhita, the International Association of Buddhist Women, have been instrumental in raising awareness about the challenges faced by women in the Sangha and promoting initiatives to support their education and empowerment. These efforts have helped to create a global network of support for women practitioners and have highlighted the importance of gender equality in spiritual practice.

Education and training programs have also been developed to support women in the Theravada community. These programs provide opportunities for women to study the Dharma, develop their meditation practice, and cultivate leadership skills. By equipping women with the knowledge and skills they need to succeed, these initiatives help to break down barriers and create opportunities for women to contribute meaningfully to the Theravada tradition.

The modern movement for gender equality within Theravada Buddhism reflects a growing recognition of the importance of inclusivity and diversity in spiritual practice. By advocating for the rights of women and addressing the barriers they face, these movements are helping to create a more equitable and vibrant Theravada community. The efforts to promote gender equality benefit not only women but the entire Buddhist tradition, fostering a more inclusive and compassionate spiritual landscape.

CONTRIBUTIONS OF WOMEN TO THERAVADA

Women have made significant contributions to the Theravada tradition, enriching the spiritual community with their wisdom, dedication, and insight. Throughout history, women have played a vital role as practitioners, teachers, and leaders, helping to preserve and transmit the teachings of the Buddha. Their contributions have had a lasting impact on the Theravada tradition, inspiring generations of practitioners and shaping the spiritual landscape.

One of the most significant contributions of women to Theravada Buddhism is their role in preserving and transmitting the teachings. From the early days of the tradition, women have been active participants in the spiritual community, offering their insights and understanding of the Dharma. Their teachings and writings have been preserved in the Buddhist texts, providing valuable resources for practitioners seeking to deepen their understanding of the Buddha's teachings.

Women have also played a crucial role in the development of meditation practices within the Theravada tradition. Notable female practitioners, such as Dipa Ma and Ayya Khema, have been instrumental in teaching and popularizing meditation techniques, both in traditional Theravada countries and in the West. Their teachings have inspired countless individuals to cultivate mindfulness and insight, contributing to the global spread of Theravada meditation practices.

In addition to their contributions as teachers and practitioners, women have been active advocates for social and environmental justice within the Theravada community. Many women have drawn on the principles of the Dharma to address contemporary challenges, such as poverty, inequality, and environmental degradation. By integrating the teachings of the Buddha with social activism, women have helped to create a more compassionate and just society.

The contributions of women to Theravada Buddhism highlight the potential for spiritual realization and leadership, regardless of gender. By offering their insights, teachings, and advocacy, women have enriched the tradition and contributed to its growth and development. Their dedication and resilience serve as a source of inspiration for all practitioners, demonstrating the transformative power of the Buddhist path.

FUTURE PROSPECTS

The future prospects for women in Theravada Buddhism are promising as the movement for gender equality continues to gain momentum and recognition within the tradition. With ongoing efforts to address the historical and institutional barriers that have limited women's opportunities, there is hope for a more inclusive and diverse Theravada community. By embracing gender equality, the tradition can benefit from the unique perspectives and contributions of women, fostering a more vibrant and dynamic spiritual landscape.

One of the key areas of focus for the future is the continued revival of the Bhikkhuni Sangha. As more women receive full ordination, there will be greater opportunities for them to participate fully in the monastic community and to assume leadership roles. This revival is essential for creating a more equitable and inclusive Theravada tradition, where women can contribute their insights and wisdom to the spiritual community.

Education and training programs will also play a crucial role in supporting women's participation in the Theravada tradition. By providing opportunities for women to study the Dharma, develop their meditation practice, and cultivate leadership skills, these programs can help to break down barriers and create a more supportive environment for women practitioners. The continued development of these initiatives will be essential for fostering a more inclusive and diverse Theravada community.

The future prospects for women in Theravada Buddhism are also shaped by the growing recognition of the importance of gender equality and inclusivity in spiritual practice. As more individuals and organizations advocate for the rights of women within the tradition, there is potential for significant progress in addressing the challenges and barriers they face. This advocacy is essential for creating a more equitable and compassionate Theravada community where all practitioners can thrive.

The future of women in Theravada Buddhism is bright, with ongoing efforts to promote gender equality and inclusivity within the tradition. By addressing the historical and institutional barriers that have limited women's opportunities, the tradition can become more diverse and dynamic, benefiting from the unique perspectives and contributions of women. The continued advocacy for gender equality will be essential for creating a more vibrant and compassionate Theravada community, fostering the growth and development of the tradition.

CONTEMPORARY ISSUES AND FUTURE DIRECTIONS

THERAVADA AND MODERN SCIENCE

The intersection of Theravada Buddhism and modern science presents intriguing possibilities. At first glance, these two fields might seem worlds apart. One focuses on spirituality and the inner life, while the other is grounded in empirical evidence and the material world. Yet, both seek to understand the nature of existence and the workings of the mind. In recent years, there has been a growing interest in exploring the connections between Buddhist teachings and scientific discoveries, particularly in fields such as psychology and neuroscience.

One area where Theravada Buddhism and modern science intersect is in the study of the mind. Buddhist teachings have long emphasized the importance of mindfulness and meditation in cultivating mental clarity and well-being. Modern research has shown that these practices can have significant benefits for mental health, including reducing stress, anxiety, and depression. Studies using brain imaging techniques have also demonstrated that regular meditation can lead to changes in brain structure and function, supporting the Buddhist view that the mind is malleable and capable of transformation.

The concept of impermanence, a central tenet of Theravada Buddhism, resonates with scientific understandings of the universe. The idea that all things are in a constant state of flux aligns with modern physics' view of a dynamic and ever-changing cosmos. This shared perspective encourages a sense of humility and curiosity as both Buddhists and scientists seek to explore the complexities of existence without clinging to fixed ideas or beliefs.

Another area of interest is the exploration of consciousness. Buddhist teachings offer profound insights into the nature of consciousness and the self, challenging the notion of a permanent, independent self. These ideas have sparked interest among scientists studying consciousness and cognitive processes, prompting questions about the nature of self-awareness and the boundaries of human experience. This dialogue has the potential to deepen our understanding of both the mind and the universe.

The relationship between Theravada Buddhism and modern science is one of mutual enrichment. While science offers tools and methods for exploring the material world, Buddhism provides insights into the nature of the mind and the path to inner peace. By engaging in dialogue and collaboration, these two fields can offer new perspectives on age-old questions, fostering a deeper understanding of the human experience.

SOCIALLY ENGAGED BUDDHISM

Socially engaged Buddhism is a movement that seeks to apply the principles of Buddhism to contemporary social, political, and environmental issues. This approach emphasizes the importance of compassion and action, encouraging practitioners to engage with the world and work towards positive change. In the Theravada tradition, socially engaged Buddhism draws on the teachings of the Buddha to address challenges such as poverty, inequality, and environmental degradation.

One of the key principles of socially engaged Buddhism is the practice of compassion. Practitioners are encouraged to cultivate compassion not only for themselves but also for others and the world around them. This involves developing empathy and understanding for the suffering of others and taking action to alleviate it. Socially engaged Buddhists see compassion as a guiding force for social change, inspiring individuals to work towards a more just and equitable society.

Socially engaged Buddhism also emphasizes the importance of mindfulness and awareness in addressing social issues. Practitioners are encouraged to bring mindfulness to their actions and decisions, recognizing the interconnectedness of all beings and the impact of their choices on the world. This awareness fosters a sense of responsibility and accountability, motivating individuals to engage in practices that promote well-being and sustainability.

In the Theravada tradition, socially engaged Buddhists often focus on grassroots initiatives and community-based projects. These efforts aim to address the root causes of social and environmental issues, such as poverty, education, and healthcare. By working at the local level, socially engaged Buddhists can foster a sense of community and solidarity, empowering individuals to take action and create positive change in their own lives and communities.

The movement for socially engaged Buddhism reflects a growing recognition of the importance of applying Buddhist teachings to contemporary challenges. By engaging with social, political, and environmental issues, socially engaged Buddhists are working towards a more compassionate and just world. Their efforts demonstrate the potential of the Buddhist path to inspire positive change and foster a more harmonious and sustainable future.

ENVIRONMENTAL ETHICS IN THERAVADA

Environmental ethics in Theravada Buddhism draw on the teachings of the Buddha to address the pressing ecological challenges of our time. The principles of interconnectedness, compassion, and mindfulness offer a framework for understanding our relationship with the natural world and for taking action to protect it. In recent years, there has been a growing recognition of the importance of integrating environmental ethics into Buddhist practice and teachings.

One of the key principles of environmental ethics in Theravada Buddhism is the concept of interconnectedness. The teachings emphasize the interdependence of all living beings and the natural world, highlighting the impact of our actions on the environment. This awareness fosters a sense of responsibility and stewardship, encouraging individuals to care for the planet and its resources. By recognizing the interconnectedness of all life, practitioners are inspired to make choices that promote sustainability and well-being for all beings.

Compassion is another central principle of environmental ethics in Theravada Buddhism. Practitioners are encouraged to cultivate compassion not only for other humans but also for all living beings and the planet itself. This involves developing empathy and understanding for the suffering caused by environmental degradation and taking action to alleviate it. By extending compassion to the natural world, individuals can foster a sense of care and responsibility for the environment.

Mindfulness and awareness are also essential components of environmental ethics in Theravada Buddhism. Practitioners are encouraged to bring mindfulness to their actions and decisions, recognizing the impact of their choices on the environment. This awareness fosters a sense of accountability and motivates individuals to engage in practices that promote sustainability and conservation. By cultivating mindfulness, practitioners can develop a deeper connection to the natural world and a greater appreciation for its beauty and complexity.

Incorporating environmental ethics into Theravada practice involves both individual and collective action. Practitioners are encouraged to make sustainable choices in their daily lives, such as reducing waste, conserving resources, and supporting environmentally friendly practices. At the community level, Buddhist organizations and temples can engage in environmental initiatives, such as tree planting, conservation efforts, and education programs. These collective efforts demonstrate the potential for positive change and the power of the

Buddhist community to address environmental challenges.

Environmental ethics in Theravada Buddhism offer a framework for understanding and addressing the ecological challenges of our time. By drawing on the principles of interconnectedness, compassion, and mindfulness, practitioners can develop a deeper connection to the natural world and take action to protect it. These teachings inspire individuals and communities to engage in practices that promote sustainability and well-being for all beings, fostering a more harmonious and sustainable future.

INTERFAITH DIALOGUE AND COOPERATION

Interfaith dialogue and cooperation are important aspects of Theravada Buddhism's engagement with the broader religious landscape. These efforts aim to foster mutual understanding, respect, and collaboration among different faith traditions, recognizing the shared values and common goals that unite them. By engaging in dialogue and cooperation, Theravada Buddhists can contribute to a more harmonious and interconnected world.

One of the key principles of interfaith dialogue is the recognition of shared values and common goals. While different faith traditions may have distinct beliefs and practices, they often share fundamental values such as compassion, peace, and justice. By focusing on these shared values, interfaith dialogue can foster a sense of solidarity and cooperation, encouraging individuals and communities to work together towards common goals.

Mutual understanding and respect are also essential components of interfaith dialogue. Participants are encouraged to approach dialogue with an open mind and a willingness to listen and learn from others. This involves developing empathy and understanding for different perspectives and recognizing the diversity and richness of the world's religious traditions. By fostering mutual understanding and respect, interfaith dialogue can promote tolerance and acceptance, reducing prejudice and conflict.

Collaboration and cooperation are important outcomes of interfaith dialogue. By working together on shared goals and initiatives, faith communities can leverage their collective resources and expertise to address pressing social and environmental challenges. This cooperation can take many forms, from joint service projects and advocacy efforts to educational programs and community events. By collaborating across faith lines, individuals and communities can create positive change and build a more just and compassionate world.

Interfaith dialogue and cooperation also offer opportunities for personal and spiritual growth. By engaging with other faith traditions, individuals can deepen their understanding of their own beliefs and practices, fostering greater insight and awareness. This engagement can also inspire new perspectives and approaches to spiritual practice, enriching one's own spiritual journey. Through interfaith dialogue, practitioners can cultivate a sense of interconnectedness and shared purpose, contributing to a more harmonious and inclusive world.

Interfaith dialogue and cooperation are important aspects of Theravada Buddhism's engagement with the broader religious landscape. By fostering mutual understanding, respect, and collaboration, Theravada Buddhists can contribute to a more harmonious and interconnected world. These efforts demonstrate the potential for positive change and the power of the Buddhist community to engage with the diversity and richness of the world's religious traditions.

THERAVADA AND GLOBALIZATION

Globalization has had a profound impact on Theravada Buddhism, shaping its development and dissemination in the modern world. As the world becomes increasingly interconnected, Theravada Buddhism has spread beyond its traditional roots in Southeast Asia to reach new audiences and communities worldwide. This global spread has brought both opportunities and challenges as Theravada Buddhism adapts to new cultural contexts and engages with contemporary issues.

One of the key opportunities of globalization is the increased accessibility and visibility of Theravada Buddhism. Through travel, communication, and technology, individuals worldwide have access to the teachings and practices of Theravada Buddhism. This increased accessibility has led to a growing interest in meditation, mindfulness, and other Buddhist practices, fostering a global community of practitioners and creating opportunities for cross-cultural exchange and learning.

The global spread of Theravada Buddhism has also led to new interpretations and expressions of the teachings. As practitioners engage with Theravada Buddhism in diverse cultural contexts, they bring their own perspectives and experiences to the tradition. This has led to the development of innovative approaches to practice, such as the integration of mindfulness with modern psychology and the application of Buddhist principles to social and environmental issues. These new interpretations reflect the adaptability and resilience of Theravada Buddhism in the face of change.

Globalization also presents challenges for Theravada Buddhism as it navigates the tensions between tradition and modernity. The spread of Western values and consumer culture can create conflicts with traditional Buddhist teachings and practices, prompting questions about the preservation of cultural heritage and the integrity of the tradition. Theravada communities must balance the need to adapt to changing circumstances with the preservation of their core teachings and values.

The interaction between Theravada Buddhism and globalization also raises important questions about cultural exchange and appropriation. As Theravada practices and teachings are adopted by individuals and communities worldwide, it is essential to ensure that these exchanges are respectful and equitable. This involves recognizing the contributions and insights of traditional Theravada communities and fostering a dialogue that values diversity and inclusivity.

Globalization presents both opportunities and challenges for Theravada Buddhism, as it spreads and adapts to new cultural contexts. By embracing the potential for cross-cultural exchange and learning, Theravada Buddhism can engage with contemporary issues and foster a global community of practitioners. These efforts demonstrate the resilience and adaptability of the tradition, offering a path of peace and wisdom for individuals worldwide.

LAUREN CHRISTENSEN

PRESERVING TRADITION IN THE MODERN WORLD

Preserving tradition in the modern world is a significant challenge for Theravada Buddhism as it navigates the tensions between tradition and change. The rapid pace of technological advancement, social change, and globalization has created new opportunities and challenges for the tradition. In response, Theravada communities must find ways to preserve their core teachings and values while adapting to contemporary circumstances.

One of the key challenges of preserving tradition is maintaining the integrity of the teachings and practices. As Theravada Buddhism spreads to new cultural contexts, there is a risk of dilution or distortion of the core teachings. To address this challenge, Theravada communities must prioritize the preservation of the teachings and ensure that they are transmitted accurately and authentically. This involves maintaining a strong connection to the traditional texts and practices while also embracing new interpretations and approaches.

Education and training are essential components of preserving tradition. By providing opportunities for individuals to study the teachings and develop their practice, Theravada communities can foster a deeper understanding and appreciation of the tradition. This education should be accessible and inclusive, welcoming individuals from diverse backgrounds and perspectives. By fostering a culture of learning and inquiry, Theravada communities can ensure the continuity and vitality of the tradition.

Preserving tradition also involves engaging with contemporary issues and challenges. By applying the teachings to modern contexts, Theravada communities can demonstrate the relevance and applicability of the tradition. This involves addressing social, environmental, and ethical challenges and fostering a dialogue that values diversity and inclusivity. By engaging with the world in meaningful ways, Theravada Buddhism can remain a dynamic and transformative force in the modern world.

The role of community is also essential in preserving tradition. Theravada communities provide a sense of belonging and support, fostering connections among practitioners and creating opportunities for shared practice and learning. By cultivating a strong sense of community, Theravada Buddhists can preserve the values of generosity, compassion, and interconnectedness that are at the heart of the tradition. This community spirit fosters resilience and adaptability, allowing Theravada Buddhism to thrive in the modern world.

Preserving tradition in the modern world is a significant challenge for Theravada Buddhism as it navigates the tensions between tradition and change. By maintaining the integrity of the teachings and engaging with contemporary issues, Theravada communities can ensure the continuity and vitality of the tradition. These efforts demonstrate the resilience and adaptability of Theravada Buddhism, offering a path of peace and wisdom for individuals worldwide.

VISION FOR THE FUTURE

The future of Theravada Buddhism holds great promise as the tradition continues to evolve and adapt to the changing world. With a strong foundation in the teachings of the Buddha and a commitment to mindfulness, compassion, and wisdom, Theravada Buddhism has the potential to address contemporary challenges and inspire positive change. By embracing innovation and inclusivity, the tradition can continue to thrive and offer guidance and support to individuals and communities worldwide.

One vision for the future of Theravada Buddhism is the continued integration of the teachings with contemporary science and psychology. By exploring the connections between Buddhist principles and scientific research, practitioners can deepen their understanding of the mind and the nature of consciousness. This integration has the potential to foster new insights and approaches to practice, enhancing the benefits of mindfulness and meditation for mental health and well-being.

Another vision for the future is the expansion of socially engaged Buddhism, addressing pressing social, political, and environmental issues. By applying the teachings of the Buddha to contemporary challenges, practitioners can work towards a more just and equitable world. This involves cultivating compassion and mindfulness in action, promoting social and environmental responsibility, and fostering a sense of interconnectedness and community.

The future of Theravada Buddhism also includes a commitment to gender equality and inclusivity within the tradition. By addressing the historical and institutional barriers that have limited women's opportunities, the tradition can become more diverse and vibrant. This involves supporting the ordination of women, providing opportunities for education and leadership, and fostering a culture of respect and equality. By embracing diversity and inclusivity, Theravada Buddhism can reflect the richness and complexity of the human experience.

The global spread of Theravada Buddhism offers new opportunities for cross-cultural exchange and learning. By engaging with diverse cultural contexts and perspectives, the tradition can foster a global community of practitioners united by shared values and goals. This global community can draw on the strengths and insights of different cultures and traditions, creating a more interconnected and harmonious world.

The vision for the future of Theravada Buddhism is one of resilience, adaptability, and inclusivity. By embracing innovation and addressing contemporary challenges, the tradition can continue to thrive and offer guidance and support to individuals and communities worldwide. These efforts demonstrate the transformative potential of the Buddhist path, offering a vision of peace, wisdom, and compassion for the future.

CONCLUSION

RECAP OF KEY CONCEPTS

Exploring Theravada Buddhism takes us on a journey through ancient teachings that continue to impact millions of lives today. It starts with the Buddha's core teachings, which focus on the Four Noble Truths and the Noble Eightfold Path. These are not just philosophical ideas; they offer a practical guide to understanding suffering, its causes, and the path to ending it. The Noble Eightfold Path lays out steps for ethical living, mental development, and gaining wisdom.

Meditation plays a crucial role in Theravada practice, with techniques like Samatha (calm) and Vipassana (insight) guiding practitioners toward mindfulness and insight. These practices help individuals develop concentration and understand the impermanent nature of reality. They encourage the cultivation of awareness and the observation of thoughts and feelings without judgment. Through meditation, practitioners learn to cultivate a peaceful and focused mind.

CONCLUSION

Ethical conduct, or sila, is another fundamental aspect of Theravada Buddhism. The Five Precepts guide laypeople, while monastics follow more extensive rules. These ethical guidelines emphasize non-violence, honesty, and respect for others, forming the foundation for harmonious living. Ethical conduct fosters compassion and empathy, encouraging individuals to act with integrity and kindness in all aspects of life.

The Sangha, or monastic community, serves as a living embodiment of the Buddha's teachings. Monastics dedicate their lives to studying and practicing the Dharma, providing spiritual guidance to lay practitioners. Their role in preserving and transmitting the teachings is vital to the continuity of Theravada Buddhism. The Sangha fosters a sense of community and support, encouraging individuals to pursue their spiritual journeys.

Theravada Buddhism's spread across cultures and its adaptation to contemporary issues highlight its relevance today. From interfaith dialogue to environmental ethics, the tradition offers insights into the challenges of modern life. By integrating ancient wisdom with contemporary concerns, Theravada Buddhism continues to inspire individuals and communities worldwide. Its timeless teachings offer a path of peace, compassion, and understanding for those seeking a meaningful life.

THE RELEVANCE OF THERAVADA TODAY

Theravada Buddhism remains highly relevant in today's fast-paced, interconnected world. Its teachings on mindfulness and meditation have gained widespread popularity, offering practical tools for managing stress and cultivating mental well-being. In an age of constant distraction, the practice of mindfulness helps individuals stay present and focused, fostering greater clarity and awareness. This relevance is reflected in the growing interest in mindfulness-based programs in healthcare, education, and workplaces.

The ethical teachings of Theravada Buddhism also hold significance in addressing contemporary challenges. The principles of non-violence, compassion, and respect for others provide a moral compass for navigating complex social and ethical dilemmas. In a world grappling with issues such as inequality and environmental degradation, these teachings offer a framework for responsible and compassionate action. They encourage individuals to consider the impact of their choices and to cultivate a sense of interconnectedness with others.

Theravada Buddhism's emphasis on personal transformation and inner peace resonates with those seeking meaning and purpose in their lives. In a society often focused on material success, the teachings encourage individuals to look inward and cultivate qualities such as patience, humility, and gratitude. This inward journey fosters a sense of contentment and fulfillment, promoting a balanced and harmonious way of living. By focusing on personal growth, individuals can develop greater resilience and adaptability.

The tradition's adaptability and openness to dialogue also contribute to its relevance. Theravada Buddhism has engaged in interfaith and intercultural exchanges, fostering mutual understanding and collaboration. This openness allows the tradition to evolve and remain responsive to contemporary concerns. By embracing diverse perspectives, Theravada Buddhism enriches its teachings and practices,

CONCLUSION

offering fresh insights and approaches to spiritual development.

Theravada Buddhism's relevance today lies in its ability to address the complexities of modern life with timeless wisdom and practical tools. Its teachings inspire individuals to cultivate mindfulness, compassion, and ethical conduct, fostering personal and social transformation. As individuals and communities continue to engage with the tradition, Theravada Buddhism offers a path of peace, wisdom, and understanding for a changing world.

PERSONAL REFLECTIONS ON PRACTICE

Embarking on a journey of Theravada practice invites profound personal reflection and transformation. Engaging with the teachings encourages individuals to explore their inner landscapes, examining their thoughts, emotions, and behaviors. This process of self-inquiry can be both challenging and rewarding, offering insights into the nature of the mind and the patterns that shape our lives. Through practice, individuals learn to cultivate awareness and develop a deeper understanding of themselves.

Meditation is a central component of personal practice, offering a space for stillness and introspection. As individuals sit in meditation, they may encounter a range of experiences, from restlessness and distraction to moments of clarity and peace. These experiences provide valuable opportunities for growth and learning, encouraging practitioners to observe their minds with curiosity and patience. Meditation fosters a sense of presence and acceptance, allowing individuals to navigate life's challenges with greater ease.

CONCLUSION

The practice of ethical conduct also invites personal reflection, encouraging individuals to consider the impact of their actions on themselves and others. Observing the Five Precepts offers a framework for living with integrity and compassion, fostering harmonious relationships and a sense of interconnectedness. This ethical reflection invites individuals to align their actions with their values, promoting a sense of purpose and fulfillment. By acting with kindness and respect, individuals contribute to a more compassionate world.

Engaging with the Theravada teachings invites individuals to explore the nature of suffering and the path to liberation. The Four Noble Truths provide a framework for understanding the causes of suffering and the possibility of freedom from it. Through practice, individuals develop insights into the nature of desire, attachment, and impermanence, cultivating a sense of equanimity and acceptance. This exploration of suffering and liberation inspires individuals to cultivate qualities such as patience, wisdom, and compassion.

The journey of Theravada practice is one of continuous reflection and growth, offering insights into the nature of the mind and the potential for transformation. By engaging with the teachings and practices, individuals develop a deeper understanding of themselves and the world around them. This personal reflection fosters a sense of connection and purpose, inspiring individuals to live with greater mindfulness, compassion, and wisdom.

CONCLUSION

CHALLENGES AND OPPORTUNITIES FOR PRACTITIONERS

Practicing Theravada Buddhism in the modern world presents both challenges and opportunities for practitioners seeking to integrate the teachings into their daily lives. The fast-paced nature of contemporary society, with its constant demands and distractions, can make it challenging to maintain a consistent practice. Balancing work, family, and social commitments with the demands of spiritual practice requires discipline, dedication, and creativity.

One of the primary challenges practitioners face is finding time for meditation and mindfulness. The busyness of modern life often leaves little room for quiet reflection and stillness. Practitioners must find ways to incorporate practice into their routines, whether through short meditation sessions, mindful breathing exercises, or integrating mindfulness into everyday activities. By making practice a priority, individuals can cultivate a sense of presence and balance amidst the demands of daily life.

Another challenge is the tendency to become discouraged or impatient with the pace of progress in practice. The path of spiritual development is often slow and incremental, requiring persistence and patience. Practitioners may encounter obstacles such as restlessness, doubt, or frustration, which can lead to feelings of discouragement. Embracing these challenges as opportunities for growth and learning can help individuals develop resilience and perseverance.

Despite these challenges, the modern world offers unique opportunities for practitioners to engage with the teachings and expand their understanding. The accessibility of resources such as books, online courses, and meditation apps provides individuals with a wealth of information and support. This access to diverse teachings and perspectives allows practitioners to explore different approaches to practice and find methods that resonate with them.

The global reach of Theravada Buddhism also offers opportunities for connection and community. Practitioners can participate in retreats, workshops, and online forums, connecting with others who share their commitment to the path. These communities provide a sense of support and encouragement, fostering a sense of belonging and shared purpose. By engaging with a global network of practitioners, individuals can draw on the collective wisdom and experience of the Theravada tradition.

Practicing Theravada Buddhism in the modern world presents both challenges and opportunities for individuals seeking to integrate the teachings into their lives. By navigating these challenges with resilience and creativity, practitioners can cultivate a sense of balance, presence, and purpose. These efforts demonstrate the transformative potential of the Theravada path, offering a way to live with greater mindfulness, compassion, and wisdom.

FUTURE DIRECTIONS FOR RESEARCH

As Theravada Buddhism continues to engage with the modern world, there are numerous opportunities for research and exploration. These future directions offer the potential to deepen our understanding of the tradition and its relevance to contemporary challenges. By exploring new areas of inquiry, researchers can contribute to the development of Theravada Buddhism and its impact on individuals and communities worldwide.

One area of interest for future research is the integration of Theravada teachings with contemporary psychology and neuroscience. Exploring the connections between Buddhist principles and scientific research can provide new insights into the nature of the mind and the benefits of meditation and mindfulness practices. This research has the potential to enhance our understanding of mental health and well-being, offering practical tools for individuals seeking to cultivate resilience and emotional balance.

Another promising direction for research is the exploration of socially engaged Buddhism and its application to social and environmental challenges. By examining the ways in which Theravada principles can be applied to issues such as poverty, inequality, and climate change, researchers can contribute to the development of innovative approaches to social change. This research highlights the relevance of the tradition to contemporary issues and demonstrates its potential for positive impact.

The study of interfaith dialogue and cooperation is another important area for research. By examining the ways in which Theravada Buddhism engages with other religious traditions, researchers can explore the potential for collaboration and mutual understanding. This research fosters a sense of inclusivity and interconnectedness, promoting dialogue and cooperation across cultural and religious boundaries.

Research into the cultural adaptations and global spread of Theravada Buddhism also offers valuable insights. By examining the ways in which the tradition is practiced and understood in different cultural contexts, researchers can explore the diversity and richness of Theravada Buddhism. This research contributes to a broader understanding of the tradition and its potential for cross-cultural exchange and learning.

Future directions for research in Theravada Buddhism offer the potential to deepen our understanding of the tradition and its relevance to contemporary challenges. By exploring new areas of inquiry, researchers can contribute to the development of Theravada Buddhism and its impact on individuals and communities worldwide. These efforts demonstrate the resilience and adaptability of the tradition, offering a path of peace and wisdom for a changing world.

RESOURCES FOR FURTHER STUDY

For those interested in deepening their understanding of Theravada Buddhism, there are numerous resources available for further study. These resources offer a wealth of information and support for individuals seeking to explore the teachings and practices of the tradition. By engaging with these resources, individuals can develop a deeper appreciation for the richness and diversity of Theravada Buddhism.

Books and texts are valuable resources for exploring the teachings of Theravada Buddhism. The Pali Canon, the primary scripture of the tradition, offers a comprehensive collection of the Buddha's teachings and discourses. Many translations and commentaries are available, providing insights into the core principles and practices of the tradition. In addition to the Pali Canon, numerous books by contemporary teachers and scholars offer accessible introductions and explorations of Theravada Buddhism.

CONCLUSION

Online courses and lectures provide opportunities for individuals to engage with the teachings in a structured and interactive format. Many organizations and institutions offer courses on various aspects of Theravada Buddhism, from meditation and mindfulness to ethics and philosophy. These courses allow individuals to learn from experienced teachers and connect with a global community of practitioners.

Meditation centers and retreats offer opportunities for individuals to deepen their practice and experience the teachings in a supportive environment. Many centers offer retreats and workshops on meditation and mindfulness, providing guidance and instruction for practitioners at all levels. These experiences allow individuals to immerse themselves in the practice and connect with others who share their commitment to the path.

Community and support groups provide opportunities for individuals to connect with others who share their interest in Theravada Buddhism. Many temples and meditation centers offer regular gatherings and events, fostering a sense of community and belonging. Online forums and social media groups also offer spaces for individuals to connect, share experiences, and seek support and guidance.

Resources for further study in Theravada Buddhism offer a wealth of information and support for individuals seeking to deepen their understanding of the tradition. By engaging with these resources, individuals can explore the teachings and practices of Theravada Buddhism and develop a deeper appreciation for its richness and diversity. These efforts demonstrate the transformative potential of the Theravada path, offering a way to live with greater mindfulness, compassion, and wisdom.

FINAL THOUGHTS AND INSPIRATIONS

Reflecting on the journey through Theravada Buddhism, one is struck by the depth and richness of the tradition. Its teachings offer timeless wisdom and practical tools for navigating the complexities of modern life. From the Buddha's core teachings on the nature of suffering and the path to liberation, to the practices of meditation and ethical conduct, Theravada Buddhism provides a comprehensive framework for personal and spiritual growth.

The resilience and adaptability of Theravada Buddhism are evident in its ability to engage with contemporary challenges and inspire positive change. From its integration with modern science and psychology to its application to social and environmental issues, the tradition offers fresh perspectives and innovative approaches to practice. By embracing diversity and inclusivity, Theravada Buddhism reflects the richness and complexity of the human experience.

The journey of Theravada practice invites individuals to explore their inner landscapes and cultivate qualities such as mindfulness, compassion, and wisdom. This journey is one of continuous reflection and growth, offering insights into the nature of the mind and the potential for transformation. By engaging with the teachings and practices, individuals can develop a deeper understanding of themselves and the world around them.

The potential for Theravada Buddhism to inspire and transform lives is vast, offering a path of peace, wisdom, and

CONCLUSION

compassion for those seeking a meaningful life. By embracing the teachings and engaging with the challenges and opportunities of the modern world, individuals can contribute to a more just and harmonious society. The Theravada path offers a vision of hope and inspiration, guiding individuals toward a more compassionate and interconnected world.

As we reflect on the journey through Theravada Buddhism, we are reminded of the power of the teachings to inspire and transform. The tradition offers a path of peace and wisdom, inviting individuals to cultivate mindfulness, compassion, and ethical conduct. By embracing the teachings and engaging with the world, practitioners can contribute to a more just and compassionate society, fostering a vision of hope and inspiration for the future.

GLOSSARY

Abhidhamma Pitaka: A collection of texts in the Pali Canon, focusing on philosophical and psychological analysis of Buddhist teachings.

Anatta: The concept of "non-self," which states that there is no permanent, unchanging soul or self in living beings.

Anicca: The concept of impermanence, emphasizing that all things are in a constant state of change and flux.

Bhikkhu: A fully ordained male monk in the Theravada Buddhist monastic community.

Bhikkhuni: A fully ordained female nun in the Theravada Buddhist monastic community.

Bodhi Tree: The sacred tree under which the Buddha attained enlightenment.

Dana: The practice of generosity and giving, considered a fundamental virtue in Buddhism.

GLOSSARY

Dhamma: The teachings of the Buddha, often referred to as the truth or law governing the universe.

Dukkha: The concept of suffering or dissatisfaction, which is a central focus in Buddhist teachings.

Eightfold Path: The path to liberation from suffering, consisting of eight practices: right view, right intention, right speech, right action, right livelihood, right effort, right mindfulness, and right concentration.

Enlightenment: The state of awakening or liberation from the cycle of birth and death, characterized by the realization of ultimate truth.

Four Noble Truths: The core teachings of the Buddha, outlining the nature of suffering, its cause, its cessation, and the path leading to its cessation.

Jhana: A meditative state of deep concentration and absorption.

Kamma: The principle of cause and effect, where actions have consequences that determine future experiences.

Karuna: The practice of compassion and empathy for the suffering of others.

Kathina: A traditional ceremony where laypeople offer robes and other necessities to monks at the end of the monastic retreat season.

Layperson: A non-ordained follower of Buddhism who supports the monastic community and practices the teachings in daily life.

GLOSSARY

Mahayana: A major branch of Buddhism emphasizing the collective liberation of all beings and the ideal of the bodhisattva.

Metta: The practice of loving-kindness and goodwill toward all beings.

Mindfulness: The practice of being fully present and aware in each moment, without judgment or distraction.

Nibbana: The ultimate goal of Theravada Buddhism, representing liberation from the cycle of rebirth and the cessation of suffering.

Noble Eightfold Path: See Eightfold Path.

Pali Canon: The authoritative scriptures of Theravada Buddhism, written in the Pali language, consisting of the Vinaya Pitaka, Sutta Pitaka, and Abhidhamma Pitaka.

Parinirvana: The final passing away of the Buddha after attaining enlightenment, marking the end of the cycle of birth and death.

Puja: A ritual offering or devotional practice performed to honor the Buddha or other spiritual beings.

Rebirth: The belief in the cycle of birth, death, and rebirth, where beings are born into new existences based on their karma.

Samadhi: A state of deep concentration and mental absorption achieved through meditation.

Samatha: A form of meditation practice focused on developing calmness and concentration.

GLOSSARY

Sangha: The community of monks, nuns, and lay practitioners who follow the teachings of the Buddha.

Sila: The practice of ethical conduct and moral discipline, forming the foundation for spiritual development.

Stupa: A mound-like structure containing relics or sacred objects, often serving as a place of meditation and devotion.

Sutta Pitaka: A collection of discourses attributed to the Buddha, forming part of the Pali Canon.

Theravada: The oldest surviving school of Buddhism, emphasizing the teachings and practices found in the Pali Canon.

Three Marks of Existence: The three characteristics of all phenomena: impermanence (anicca), suffering (dukkha), and non-self (anatta).

Tripitaka: See Pali Canon.

Uposatha: Observance days in Theravada Buddhism, marked by intensified practice and adherence to precepts.

Vassa: The annual monastic retreat season during the rainy months, where monks and nuns focus on study and meditation.

Vesak: A major Buddhist festival celebrating the birth, enlightenment, and passing of the Buddha.

Vinaya Pitaka: The section of the Pali Canon that contains the monastic code and rules of discipline for monks and nuns.

Vipassana: A form of meditation practice focused on developing insight into the nature of reality.

GLOSSARY

Wheel of Dharma: A symbol representing the teachings of the Buddha and the path to enlightenment.

Zen: A school of Mahayana Buddhism emphasizing meditation and direct insight into the nature of reality.

Zazen: A form of seated meditation practiced in Zen Buddhism, focusing on mindfulness and concentration.

Zazen: A form of seated meditation practiced in Zen Buddhism, focusing on mindfulness and concentration.

Zendo: A meditation hall in a Zen monastery where practitioners gather for meditation and practice.

Zhaozhou: A famous Chinese Zen master known for his teachings and koans, emphasizing direct insight and spontaneous wisdom.

Zhuangzi: An ancient Chinese philosopher whose writings are associated with Daoism, exploring themes of spontaneity, harmony, and the nature of reality.

Zhengyi: A school of Daoism emphasizing ritual practice, meditation, and the cultivation of virtue and harmony with nature.

Zhiyi: A Chinese Buddhist monk and founder of the Tiantai school, known for his teachings on meditation, the nature of reality, and the integration of Buddhist philosophy.

Zither: A musical instrument with strings, often used in traditional Asian music, and associated with cultural and spiritual practices.

SUGGESTED READINGS

Ajahn Brahm - *Mindfulness, Bliss, and Beyond: A Meditator's Handbook*

Ajahn Chah - *Food for the Heart: The Collected Teachings of Ajahn Chah*

Bhikkhu Bodhi - *In the Buddha's Words: An Anthology of Discourses from the Pali Canon*

Bhikkhu Bodhi - *The Noble Eightfold Path: Way to the End of Suffering*

Buddhadasa Bhikkhu - *Heartwood of the Bodhi Tree: The Buddha's Teaching on Voidness*

Joseph Goldstein - *Mindfulness: A Practical Guide to Awakening*

Joseph Goldstein - *The Experience of Insight: A Simple and Direct Guide to Buddhist Meditation*

Jack Kornfield - *Living Buddhist Masters*

SUGGESTED READINGS

Jack Kornfield - *The Path of Insight Meditation*

Henepola Gunaratana - *Mindfulness in Plain English*

Henepola Gunaratana - *Beyond Mindfulness in Plain English: An Introductory Guide to Deeper States of Meditation*

Thich Nhat Hanh - *The Heart of the Buddha's Teaching: Transforming Suffering into Peace, Joy, and Liberation*

Nyanaponika Thera - *The Heart of Buddhist Meditation: Satipatthana: A Handbook of Mental Training Based on the Buddha's Way of Mindfulness*

Nyanatiloka Thera - *The Word of the Buddha: An Outline of the Buddha's Teaching in the Words of the Pali Canon*

Sarah Shaw - *Buddhist Meditation: An Anthology of Texts from the Pali Canon*

Stephen Batchelor - *Buddhism Without Beliefs: A Contemporary Guide to Awakening*

Steve Hagen - *Buddhism Plain and Simple*

Thanissaro Bhikkhu - *The Wings to Awakening: An Anthology from the Pali Canon*

Thanissaro Bhikkhu - *The Paradox of Becoming: Identity and Continuity in Buddhist Thought*

Walpola Rahula - *What the Buddha Taught*

Printed in Great Britain
by Amazon